Disturbi

George Lee Hunter

Table of Contents

Dedication

This book is dedicated to my mother, Karen Shayne Hunter. Your unconditional love and never saying no to helping with my success is why I was able to accomplish so much. Thank you for believing in me.

All my love.

Acknowledgments

I would like to acknowledge my sister Lynn Hunter for reigniting my fire several times before it became organic.

I would also like to express my gratitude to Savvy Book Publishing for assisting me with putting my ideas and imagination on paper.

About the Author

As a young boy, George endured a life of abuse and torment. As a result of this upbringing, George developed terrifying dreams that would spill into reality as he awoke just for a few seconds. Those few seconds terrified him on many occasions, and he often focused on it at school, which diminished his ability to learn. As he aged, the dreams disappeared but not the sensation which compelled him to write this novel.

Chapter One

The most difficult part about writing, in my opinion, is how to begin. How do I tell the world this fascinating yet unbelievable story? I feel no matter how I come across, people will go on believing whatever helps them sleep. Unfortunately for me, that's where my problems began.

I turned twenty-nine when I invented it. I had no idea what I stumbled upon and underestimated the gravity and complexity it entailed. Before I go into the specifics, I first, like any good writer, need to start at the beginning. I just attained my master's in psychology, where my main focus was sleep deprivation and dream psychology. Not the most recognized field out there, I know, but I strongly believe that dreams can be manipulated through hypnosis. My thesis proved that communicating with subjects while they slept could actually calm night terrors. Out of twenty patients, 75% said their nightmares were no longer an issue. Out of those 75%, all of their spouses said they no longer have to defend themselves while they slept. I actually found that quite amusing. I graduated with honors which prompted me to open up my own practice, where I began treating people that were suffering from night terrors.

My first patient was a twenty-four-year-old woman named Jasmine Clyde. Our first encounter led me to believe that she was withdrawn and extremely depressed. She also had a timid way about her which kept her guarded during the sessions. I found her to be quite intelligent and very stimulating. Professionally, of course. Not that I wasn't attracted, she was a very beautiful woman, but I take my profession very seriously. Jasmine came to me concerned due to having trouble sleeping. Also, when she could sleep, she would have this recurring nightmare of falling to her death. The dreams began a year prior to her coming to see me.

At first, her dreams haunted her occasionally; she explained that when she woke from her dreams, she would get up, race to the bathroom, splash water on her face, then sit in the living room and watch TV until she fell asleep again. A few months went by with her repeating the same routine, coping the only way she knew how.

Jasmine told me of an event that happened to her that I thought was relevant. It was Valentine's Day which excited her. Her boyfriend had made reservations at this five-star restaurant where she was sure he was going to propose. All she envisioned that day was their future wedding. He made plans to pick her up at 7 pm that night, but Jasmine couldn't wait, being the spontaneous type. Instead of waiting for the night to arrive, she decided to save him a trip and took a train to his place. She hopped the train, which conveniently dropped her off a block away. She wanted to surprise him with a fast roll in the hay before the night, hoping it would guarantee it would go exactly as she anticipated. With a spare key he gave her, she quietly opened the door and let herself in.

Tiptoeing toward the bedroom, she realized he was not alone. Her heart immediately began to race. Her eyes started filling up with tears even before she could see inside. All her instincts screamed that he was with another woman. She was enraged. Being the woman Jasmine is, she wouldn't let a tramp get away from confronting the scumbag until she peered inside. She couldn't believe what she had witnessed. The scumbag was in bed with her sister. Jasmine's sister had always been jealous, but this was beyond cruel. Completely broken, Jasmine backed away from the door and dropped to her knees. She remembered covering her face with her hands to muffle the intense sobbing. A ticklish laugh bellowed from the bedroom. Jasmine swiftly removed her hands away from her face. Fearing she would be seen, she stood up and quickly hurried out the front door. She couldn't believe the future she envisioned with this creep was gone. In her crucial state, she still managed to catch her train and get herself home.

She stormed into her house, slammed the door behind her, and ran into her bedroom, where she smothered herself with her pillow. She mournfully closed her swollen eyes and fell into a deep sleep. That night, she had the most vivid nightmare she had yet to experience. The way Jasmine explained, it seemed to genuinely terrify her, which was easy to deduce due to the expressions on her face. The dream began with her in an elevator which seemed to always head to the top floor. The door would open, and, like always, she would step out. When she turned back toward the elevator, it was gone. Completely vanished. When she again faced forward, the building that she was once standing in would also be gone. The only thing in front of her now was a long, narrow sidewalk that seemed to go on forever. At that point, she would cautiously proceed forward, treading carefully, not knowing what to expect. Not long after, Jasmine peered back to record her progress but realized the sidewalk she previously trod on was crumbling and catching up to her. That prompted her to move quickly. She recalled it as running like the wind. It was never fast enough, though, she explained. The crumbling concrete always caught up with her, at which point she would fall, racing toward the earth, feeling utterly helpless. Just before she hit the ground, like always, she would wake up, screaming and crying. She managed to pull herself together, again and again, and run to the washroom to drench her face with water. But that night was different than any other, and she knew it. Jasmine stated that even though she was awake, she still felt the sensation of falling. She explained that ever since that night, like clockwork, the nightmare was waiting.

Seven long months went by before she decided to seek help, which is when she contacted me.

Chapter Two

It didn't take long before I acquired my second patient. Samuel Adams III was his name. I made the mistake of calling him Sam on one occasion, which agitated him more than it probably should have. He came across as quite pretentious at first, but listening to him talk about his upbringing made me believe it was more of a defense mechanism. It kept people at arm's length.

Samuel was forty-two years young. He was married with two children and was also an airline pilot for Sky Gliders America. He came to me because of a recurring nightmare of a plane crash. He said the helplessness he felt when he was dreaming was now spilling into his personal life. Samuel's dream was a popular night terror that many people have experienced, but he seemed to have more of an impact on me due to him being a pilot himself.

Samuel had been flying for over fifteen years. It seemed to me that he was having a midlife crisis, and his dreams resulted from his burnout. I recommended he take a leave of absence while we were in session. He was reluctant at first, but after some convincing on my part, he understood that it was the best course of action.

Samuel was the first patient I hypnotized without supervision. I treaded cautiously for the first few sessions because even though I performed hypnotism on hundreds of subjects, I was feeling both excited and nervous. There was always a chance of something going wrong when putting a patient under. The sessions went pretty much as planned. Actually, they were quite underwhelming. All Samuel did was sleep. There were no episodes of his nightmare, nor could I get him to respond to my voice while he was under. The fourth meeting was completely different. We finally had a breakthrough. As the tormented man slept, all I could make out was him exclaiming that he couldn't help. "There's nothing I can do!" he screamed. "There's nothing I can do!" I only reassured him that everything was fine and he needn't worry about not helping. Everything was fine, and he was in a safe place.

When Samuel awoke, he was teary-eyed but saw me and immediately felt relieved to be in my office. He began to explain a moment in his dream where he felt in control. He heard my voice, and immediately a calm washed over him. I was impressed. I made contact. Plus, for the first time, Samuel thought there might be a solution to his crisis.

We went on for weeks trying to recreate the last successful encounter but to no avail. I felt his frustration growing, and I was agitated as well. But there was nothing more I could do unless we interacted while he slept. The poor man's night terrors persisted, but no communication happened. I realized I needed a new approach to his situation. Also, to bide my time until I figured out what approach that would be. Second-guessing myself was what led me in the direction of building the machine, which we will get to very soon.

Samuel and I discussed my leave of absence so I could come up with new strategies. He wouldn't see me for close to five weeks. At that time, I acquired three new patients plus Jasmine. I was keeping myself so busy that I actually forgot about Samuel. Plus, during my hiatus, I came up with this exciting idea that was occupying all of my time at home.

Chapter Three

I was taking a shower when it came to me; I needed to somehow interact with my patients while they slept, and so far had been unsuccessful. The direction I was taking seemed to be ineffective, and I needed a new approach. It was only a matter of time before my patients realized I was stalling. That's when it hit me, literally hit me, *water!* Water was the answer. Water was the perfect conduit to link my subjects and me together while we slept.

At first, I envisioned a big pool with all my patients floating as I talked with them about their parents. *I guess that would make me a marine psychologist*, I thought, which made me chuckle. Water alone would do nothing, but if I introduced small currents of electricity to the water, it could theoretically link us.

I recalled watching a movie as a child. It had to do with deprivation chambers. There were these huge box-shaped vessels that resembled washing machines. I began to envision myself lying in one with my subjects in the other; water surrounding our entire bodies as we lightly bob up and down. The chamber doors closed from the top automatically, darkness slowly engulfing us. A needle sneaks up and pricks our neck, injecting a sleep induced, which would be administered after they were hypnotized. The machine then would introduce low current electricity to the water, which would pulsate through our bodies. Microphones installed on both sides of the interior of the chamber would communicate back and forth. While the subjects drifted away, I would begin the most crucial part of the process, which was getting my subjects in the right state of mind before they fell completely asleep. I truly believed this would work. I just underestimated how well.

I quickly got on the computer to find parts for this genius plan of mine. It was uncanny what you could find on the internet. There were more than a hundred hits on deprivation chambers alone. Four seemed to be the magic number due to a sale. A sale on deprivation chambers! That made me laugh. 'All must go', it wrote, 'four deprivation chambers for the price of one!' I wasn't too big on fate, but this seemed to just fall into place. The picture on the net didn't look like any of the chambers I have ever seen. These were stainless steel, cylindrical masterpieces. I was completely captivated and put a rush on order immediately, which was delivered within days. At that point, I needed a technician to help out with putting schematics together. That was when I met Will Livingston. I picked will due to his personal life. He lived alone with his dog Teeny. Should've seen this pup. I held it in one hand. A beautiful, tanned, teacup Chihuahua. Will had no children and was married to his career. He was by far the most skilled individual I knew. I can't explain exactly what he did, but the machine we built worked extraordinarily. My main concern was the project and his anonymity. I truly had no business building the machine without approval from the psychiatric board. I could've got into serious trouble. Events were moving so fast that I really didn't think of the repercussions, or maybe just didn't care. I was so eager to prove my theory that I'm not sure if God himself could've convinced me to quit.

I explained to Will exactly what I was thinking. Without hesitation, he grasped the concept! It took Will a couple of days to draw diagrams, but when I saw what he had done, I was astounded at how accurate they were. It was like he could see what I envisioned. Will and I became close very quickly. It seemed we had a lot in common – work came first for both of us. There were times Will and I worked right through the night, which convinced me that Will's attraction to this project was as great as mine.

When the deprivation chambers arrived, I was absolutely giddy. The pictures on the net did not do these magnificent vessels justice. They were so futuristic, bright, stainless steel, which cast my reflection. I remember it clearly because when I saw myself, I recalled smiling as I rarely smiled. All day I caught myself laughing and grinning from ear to ear. I called Will on his cellphone, pleading for him to come as quick as he could, but he was on a server's call for the next few hours, so I had to wait. All I remember doing for all that time was staring into these stainless steel metal coverings of the exterior of the chambers, imagining I was peering into another world and the wonders it held.

Will eventually arrived in the evening. I greeted him at the door as I quickly ushered him down to the basement. I thought the basement was a perfect place to hold our sessions. There were 2200 square feet to work with. Ten-foot-high ceilings, and I had a chandelier that illuminated the whole left side of the basement, which would be our work area. Not to mention my pool table and the full bar on the right side. I also put up blue wallpaper, which in my opinion, made the whole room come together. Will and I worked tirelessly that night. We left the chambers until last due to them being so heavy, but when we got around to organizing them, we positioned them initially in a way that morbidly resembled coffins all lined up side by side. We both just stared at each other in disgust, then at each other with this eerie look on our faces. We were both prompted to laugh. Both exhausted, we chuckled and finished up. We then decided to move two of them, so there were two rows of two.

Chapter Four

Before I knew it, weeks had gone by. My patients had been neglected, and my answering machine was flooded with messages full of profanity, asking me to phone them back. I guess I should've been relieved my patients cared enough to curse me out.

The first patient I phoned was Jasmine Clyde. I could feel that she was upset with me, but because of her kind nature, she tried to mask her discontent. I began by apologizing and then went into the work that kept me so busy. I explained that we were about to begin radical therapy. It was up to her if she wanted to participate, but if she chose to, a waiver would need to be signed as well as a disclosure agreement. Jasmine was more than happy to agree; she knew it was better than the alternative.

After speaking with Jasmine, I contacted Samuel and the rest of my patients. Samuel decided to curse me out for ten minutes, but just like the rest of them, he came around and agreed.

I decided the experiment would be controlled by Will and myself. It would take a week to set up, and the clock was now ticking. And Will, at that very moment, was at my house, making sense of the electrical components. That was the final piece of the puzzle before the first test run, and if all went according to plan, Will assured me that we would be ready for the first group of subjects by Sunday.

I remember vividly that Will came charging into my room, flicked on the light, and began screaming for me to get the hell up. I tried to ignore him by draping the pillow over my face due to me being utterly exhausted, but that techie was a persistent one. When screaming failed, he boldly began to jump on my bed like an eight-year-old child. I knew then that he was not going away. Plus, I had a strong inclination that he completed his work and was unable to contain his excitement. I tore the pillow from my face and attempted to give him a scowl but was unable to contain my smile. Will's noticeable smile forced my hand, which prompted me to laugh. He wouldn't even let me go to the washroom! I lunged out of bed, grabbed my robe, and was forced to the basement.

When I first laid eyes on what he had created, I was mesmerized. It was this futuristic control station. The way it was set up resembled Sulu's control station in this new Star Trek movie. There were so many switches and blinking lights it made me feel like a kid in a candy store. I propped myself down in front of this futuristic toy, feeling absolutely overwhelmed. Everything in front of me looked so foreign; I knew I wouldn't be able to work this machinery alone. I took that opportunity to ask Will if he would assist me further with the experiment, but before I could utter the words, Will assured me that it all looked more complicated than it actually was. His pep talk did little to comfort me. Will needed to be the operator. There was no question.

I raced upstairs and snagged my checkbook. I wanted to pay Will what I owed him before anything else was decided. When I handed the check over, he just smiled. I thanked him for his services and then shook his hand. Will thanked me for everything, then headed toward the stairs to leave. All I remember was yelping out this pathetic geeky squeak, "Wait, Will!" I screamed. He turned out laughing and asked what the hell I just said. As embarrassed as I felt at that moment, I was still able to proceed to ask him to assist me. I trusted him; he knew the machine well, and if anything went wrong, who better to be at the controls than the very one who built the damn thing?

Will was more than pleased to accept the job. He expressed to me how proud he was of the project and wanted to run it. He then explained that he would participate on the condition that no one touches the controls but him. He was adamant about overseeing all maintenance. I knew it was due to him feeling like this was his baby.

We were finally ready for the next step, which was the test run. Will needed to calibrate the electrical current which would flow through the water, and with me being the only one there with him, I became the guinea pig.

Will, trying to be the funny man, asked me in this terrible Spock impersonation, "Want to take a ride, captain?"

I didn't. At all. All I could do at first was stare, stare at that stainless steel tube with my reflection staring right back at me. Quiet filled the basement. Without notice, Will opened the pod door. The vibrations of the machine quickly reached my toes as a low-pitched humming noise flooded my ears. I turned abruptly to face Will, feeling like he was trying to rush me. Our eyes met, but all he did was nod. I remember turning back toward the chambers and taking a deep breath. I reluctantly proceeded to slip off my robe and let it fall to the floor. The time was here. It was just me, my boxers, and a date with darkness.

I shuffled over to the chambers. Only two stairs separated me from the machine. I dropped my hands on each side of the opening, and with one last gasp, I entered one leg after the other.

To my surprise, the water was quite tepid, which compelled me to submerge my entire body. I was impressed by how spacious the pod was, which immediately created a certain comfortability. I cautiously leaned back until my body was completely relaxed. I calmly lay there as all my anxieties quickly dissipated, bobbing up and down with my eyes closed. Will's voice quietly spilled through the speakers, "Are you ready, sir?" in a soft whisper.

"As I'll ever be," I replied.

Without hesitation, Will pressed the button to close the chamber door. My anxiety immediately came back with a vengeance. I was actually afraid. The capsule door quickly closed and blocked out the remainder of the light. The machine was able to monitor my heart rate, brainwaves, and breathing. It was a good thing, too, because I was panicking, which Will picked up on immediately. His voice filled the pod, asking me to calm myself.

"Everything was good," he said with a reassuring tone.

At that moment, calmness splashed over me again. Will's voice managed to soothe me and settle my rapid breathing. When he realized I had settled, he continued with the test run.

"Are you ready, sir?" he asked. "Here comes the current."

Without me answering, he pushed the button. Immediately the electricity began to flow through my entire body. The initial sensation was very uncomfortable, but soon after, it became non-existent.

Twenty minutes had passed when Will's voice filled the chambers yet again. "Everything's a go, sir."

I was completely drenched, lying in the dark, just after getting zapped by electricity, but I was ecstatic. While bobbing in the chambers, waiting to be released, I took the opportunity to express to Will how appreciative I was and couldn't possibly have done it without him.

The chamber door opened. I sat up, smiling; I looked right at Will and stated that we were ready to go... How wrong I was.

Chapter Five

Our first test run was finally complete. All that was needed now was for me to measure the correct dosage of the sleep-inducer. It was my own concoction that contained an over-the-counter sleeping aid with a drop of hypnosis.

I learned of Hypnostyle in university. A very powerful drug that people were now using for recreation on the streets. It was not hard to attain, to say the least. Not to incriminate him, but Will was well-groomed in that lifestyle. He used to have major issues with pills and cocaine but had the sense to seek help and had been clean for over four years. I could see the past lingering with him whenever I looked into his eyes. I insisted he not help me with this purchase. Will regressing back to his old ways would have been devastating. We had become good friends, and I genuinely was troubled when he insisted on helping but knew I was a square. He just didn't want me to risk getting ripped off, or worse, caught. He composed a compelling argument, so reluctantly, I agreed as long as he headed my warning not to regress or get caught himself. The coolest thing happened after that – I smoked my first reefer.

Will began telling me about his fiancé and how she died of leukemia. They never got married. Three days before the wedding, Will regrettably found her in the backyard. She'd been gardening when she passed. Will, at that point, took out the joint, "You're gonna smoke this with me," he said. I was so involved with the painful memory I couldn't refuse. He had the joint dangling from his bottom lip, finishing the story he uttered. "She loved her flowers; I'm glad she died with her flowers."

Will then reached into his pocket and pulled out an old, wooden match. With one flick of his thumb, the match ignited. I didn't say anything, but man, it was cool. I had always been a little geeky throughout my life, but at that moment, I felt like a cool kid defying his parents. Will put the flame to the joint and puffed on it a few times. The flame grew larger with each draw. He then pulled the match away and took an enormous drag. With two fingers and squinting eyes, Will pulled the joint out of his mouth. With a huge sigh, he blew out the match. An enormous cloud of smoke came barreling out of his mouth, which surrounded me instantly. I remember letting out a reserved cough. Will smiled and handed me the joint. Me being the geek I was, I grabbed it awkwardly out of his hand and dropped it on the floor. So much for looking cool. He didn't say anything. I rushed to pick it up and took a fast drag. As I inhaled it, I felt the smoke immediately heat my lungs. I'm not sure if it was the weed or lack of oxygen, but releasing the smoke from my lungs and watching it spill over everything was one of the coolest things I ever saw. I don't remember anything else about that night.

The first real session happened on August 9th, 2012. Two days after my drug experience. I got in contact with Vanessa first. Out of all my patients, she was the only one who picked up.

Vanessa was another patient of mine suffering from night terrors. Her dreams were about being eaten alive by wild animals. Vanessa and I had not had a session for a couple of weeks, so you can imagine how relieved she was to hear from me. I explained that the new direction we were about to take with our sessions was up and ready to go. I asked her to arrive at my place by 3 pm the following day for a consultation. Vanessa arrived at my house right at three. Just by looking at her, I could see she was absolutely exhausted. I felt I was partially to blame. I knew it was due to her restless sleep. I helped remove her jacket and asked how she was feeling. She responded by saying she was fine, but I knew she was covering.

There was no time to waste. We proceeded toward the basement and began explaining to her that from this point on, our sessions would take place there. When we entered the basement, I told her to make herself comfortable. She headed toward the bar and grabbed a stool. I took her for a scotch drinker. I grabbed two glasses and filled them up with ice from the ice bin. I remember thinking I gave her a very generous portion of alcohol due to her looking like she needed it. It wasn't normally how my sessions began, and I explained that since it was only an introduction to the chambers, it seemed harmless.

We took our drinks and walked over to the chambers. By that time, I knew how to open the pod. After she didn't appear to exude any agitation, I leaned over to the console and pressed open. With the pod door sliding open, I observed Vanessa's body language very closely. She didn't appear to exude any agitation in the slightest. If anything, she looked eager to begin.

The pod doors had completely opened. Vanessa, without hesitation, walked over and peered in. Staring at her reflection in the water, she placed her hand in the pod, submerging it gently, caressing the water. She looked back at me; with a courageous tone, she demanded to know, "When."

"Soon," I told her. "When all my patients were up to speed, we would begin. It would take a day or two at least."

I recall at that moment, Vanessa began to cry. She couldn't hold back anymore. She expressed her fear and couldn't take another night of being terrorized. I reassured her that everything was gonna be fine. We would begin soon enough. Looking like she felt better, Vanessa took one last swig of her scotch, gave me a huge embrace, and proceeded to leave.

After escorting Vanessa to the door, the phone rang. Samuel had received the message I had left earlier. I left no specifics except to phone me back when he could. He was relieved when I told him the experiment was ready to go. I asked him to come by for counsel so we could go through the details as I did with Vanessa. I wanted to meet him that night, but it being so late in the evening, he declined. Samuel had to get his kids off to school, so we settled for 9 am the following day.

It was around 9 in the evening when Jasmine called. She had just returned from work where she was waitressing. Her voice sounded weak. I could hear she was completely exhausted. Jasmine asked what my message was pertaining to. When I told her everything was ready and we just needed to get together to discuss the specifics, she was happy, to say the least. She began to explain that she had been taking Benzedrine and had been up for days. I tried to set up an appointment for the following day, but she explained that work kept her very busy. Then she asked if she could come over immediately. I have to admit the first thing that crossed my mind was unprofessional. Jasmine was very attractive, and it was late. I knew she worked late evenings, and there was no other time that we could meet. Plus, I wanted to begin the experiments as soon as possible, so I agreed.

It took Jasmine forty-five minutes to arrive with her living uptown and me in the suburbs. I knew the moment she was close. Her car would tip me off and made this clinking noise the whole neighborhood could hear. This girl was struggling in every way; it made me feel more than pleased to have the opportunity to try and change her life.

Jasmine arrived wearing a black, strapless dress. Her hair was pulled back, sort of revealing the curves of her neck. I was puzzled as to why she was dressed up. I knew she had just finished working. Instead of making it an issue, I just welcomed her in and complimented her. She just smiled and politely thanked me. I escorted her downstairs to the basement. While she walked down, I caught myself glancing. She was stunning. We got downstairs, and I raced to the bar. I wanted to put something between us due to it being so late and me not fully trusting myself. I asked her to sit down and offered her a drink. She pulled up the stool and asked for a whiskey neat. I looked up at her and smiled, thinking she was kidding, but quickly realized she was dead serious. I remember she gave me this empty smile like she was giving up and then slowly lowered her head so I couldn't see her tearing eyes. I immediately filled the dead air with a question and asked if she knew what those were, motioning to the deprivation chambers.

Remembering our conversation from a few weeks back, she wiped her eyes and replied, "Are those the chambers?"

I was impressed that she paid attention. "Yes," I replied. Walked up from behind the bar, I proceeded toward the chambers. Jasmine is following right behind. I walked up to the console and again pressed the only button I knew how to operate – the open button. Jasmine quickly turned, following the humming noise. While watching the doors open, she cautiously proceeded toward them. The stainless steel chambers captured her modeled reflection, growing with every step. When she reached the chambers, she brushed her hands over the smooth texture, eventually reaching the opening. Staring into the dark chamber seemed to make her a little nervous, which prompted her to ask, "How long we would have to stay in for?" At that point, I knew she was feeling apprehensive, so I began to explain how everything would be monitored. And at any moment, for any reason, the pod doors would open for her. I further explained that the very person that built the machines would also be running them. Any agitation on Jasmine's part would be addressed and dealt with before going any further.

To hear how I intended to take care of her must have triggered something because Jasmine, at that very moment, walked up to me and gave me a very passionate kiss. My heart began racing. This three-minute kiss felt like it lasted an hour. The rules I was breaking. Ethics all out the window. In theory, resisting a woman is easy; I just couldn't. Jasmine's smell was so intoxicating. Her touch was so soft. I placed my hands on each side of her neck and pulled her closer. She let out a relieving sigh, realizing I was enjoying myself just as much as she was. When we pulled our lips away, our eyes met. I asked if she was okay and if we had done anything wrong. She began telling me her attraction toward me lingered with her for a while. And that I did not just take advantage of her broken soul.

Jasmine was special. I felt so in touch with her, yet we were born eight years apart. I didn't care what anybody thought. I liked her, and I was going forward. Jasmine asked for another drink and followed me toward the bar. As I poured the whiskey, she again reassured me that she was fine. Everything was okay, I told her. And not to worry. I think that was the answer she was looking for because she then asked if she could stay the night with me. She was a bold little minx. I felt the blood rush to my face immediately.

Women were not my strong suit, but I didn't let that stop me. I placed her whiskey on the bar and slid it toward her.

"I would like that," I said in a very smooth tone, trying to stare her down. She just stared right back, smiled, and sipped her whiskey.

Chapter Six

I woke the next morning with Jasmine's arm draped over my chest. Her Chanel perfume lingered in the air. I know that intoxicating smell was hers because it sure wasn't my perfume.

As I tried to quietly shuffle out of bed, my doorbell rang. I glanced at the clock to see the time – it was 8.55 am. Samuel, being himself, was right on time.

I quickly grabbed my robe to conceal my naked body and crept out of the room, closing the squeaking door behind me. As the door squeaked, I remember cursing and raising my fist to it like it would be punished if it didn't stop that racket immediately.

I opened the door, invited Samuel in, and offered to take his hat and coat. Samuel was a very stylish dresser. This hat Samuel had come right out of a Humphrey Bogart movie, and with his jacket being a long overcoat, he resembled a detective from a 1950s movie.

I asked him to follow me to the basement, where magic was going to happen. As we headed down, he began to tell me how his dreams were getting worse. He went on; his wife was worried about him, and the last few night terrors were beginning to panic her. You can imagine how elated she was when he made the appointment.

We got downstairs and the basement smelled of Nabob. Every morning at 9, fresh coffee was waiting due to my nifty timer. I asked Samuel to sit at the bar while I made him a cup. Instead of sitting, he walked right to the chambers. When I finished pouring, I walked over to Samuel and handed him his coffee.

"So, what do you think?" I remember asking in an inquisitive tone. He had seen them once before, he told me. He knew what he was looking at.

"I liked it," he said.

He began to explain how the pods were supposed to work. I was curious about what he knew, so I listened to him talk. If he had already understood the specifics, then he wouldn't be nervous come the experiment. He was fairly accurate too. Besides the sleep-aid and the electricity, he understood completely. When I told him about the electricity, he shrieked. It bothered him a little. I then explained that I had already tried it myself, and it was completely safe. Everyone was on board. The test would begin the following day. Samuel was intrigued and couldn't wait. He was definitely in.

The basement door opened, and both Samuel and I gazed at the stairs as we watched these slender legs slowly reveal themselves. I completely forgot Jasmine was there!

She managed to find one of my lab coats and decided to follow the smell of coffee. When she reached the bottom stair, she realized I had company.

"I am so sorry!" she cried, turning around to head back upstairs. I remember calling out to her and asking her to stay. This involved all of us, I told her. It also looked like Jasmine could use a coffee.

Samuel stood up and introduced himself. Gently, he took her hand and kissed it, just like the gentleman he was. I think it made me a little jealous. Jasmine smiled, asked how he was doing, and then gently pulled her hand away. She then turned to me and sat on my lap. She wrapped her arms around my neck and kissed me gently. Jasmine politely asked if I could make her a coffee. She still looked a little tired from the night before, so I was more than happy to. I also topped Samuel and myself up as well.

We began discussing the experiment and how I wanted both of them there the following night. I also brought up Vanessa and how she was troubled and needed to be part of the experiment. They were okay with another patient and were excited to meet her. I decided, at that moment, that this would be my group. I didn't need any other patients. I was going to focus on them until I proved my theory. Will was the last piece of the puzzle, and as soon as I introduced him to the group, everything would be complete.

Jasmine took one last sip of her coffee and stood up; she had to go to work and needed a shower. She leaned over and gave me another hug, and kissed me on the cheek.

"I have to go," she explained.

I wished her a good day and told her to come by later that night if she wanted. Jasmine then waved to Samuel, said goodbye, and left. Samuel was not far behind. He shot his coffee down and said he would see me the following night. As I walked him to the door, I handed him his hat and assisted him with his coat.

As I opened the door, I remember uttering, "Until tomorrow then, sir."

"Good day," Samuel replied, then shut the door.

Now all I needed was to phone Will. He and I hadn't been in contact for a few days because I had to contact my patients. He was waiting on me to set the start date. When I phoned him, he was on the road coming back from the cemetery where he was visiting his wife. It would've been their seventh anniversary.

I explained everything was ready and told him about the group, which seemed to cheer him up. I asked him to be early the next day so that we could run things one more time before the test. Will was pumped. He had no problem with the time frame and assured me he would be there. Now all we had to do was wait.

***

It was 10 pm when my phone rang. I was asleep on my couch in the living room when I jumped up to answer it. Jasmine was phoning to see if I was serious when I asked her to come over.

"Of course, I was," I exclaimed.

The experiment would begin the next day, and I planned to stay up the entire night anyway. I told her that if she came by, it would make staying up all night much easier. Jasmine rushed over, and by the time she arrived, I had wine chilling in the living room and dimmed the lights to capture the mood.

I met Jasmine at the door; she was still wearing her waitress uniform.

"Come in," I said. She walked by me, and an overwhelming odor of beef filled my sinuses.

"I came right from work," she said. "I hope that's okay."

Everything was fine, I told her and asked if she would like to take a shower. I was hoping she would. The smell of beef was quite overwhelming. She must have also realized it because she thanked me and immediately proceeded to the washroom. I could see she hated her job. It got me wondering why she was a waitress. She must've had dreams...goals one time. What happened to this lovable creature showering in my bathroom. For her to feel so defeated, was I an escape from her hell, I wondered. I truly hope so.

I was resting on the couch when she came out. All she had was a towel wrapped around her. Still dripping, she came and sat down beside me.

"Thank you, again," she said, then leaned over and began kissing me. Her body was pushing against mine. She pushed my shoulders down with her hand, prompting me to lie back. As I lowered myself down on the couch, she straddled me. Her wet dripping auburn hair covered my face as she kissed me.

The rest of the night was magical. I had never made love like that, ever. I was completely in love with her. We drank wine, talked, and watched *Sleepless in Seattle*. She told me the first night she slept over was the first time in a while she didn't experience her night terror. It was the first good sleep she had had in months, which was the real reason she asked to stay the night. She was attracted to me and wanted to be there, but she also wanted to be honest with me. I was speechless. The girl meant the world to me. I was concerned that, on some subconscious level, she was attracted to me because she was associating her dreams with our encounter. I then cautiously asked her if being intimate with me was bothering her and if there was anything that might be drawing her to me other than her attraction. Jasmine immediately understood what I was driving at. She looked me dead in the eye and reassured me that one had nothing to do with the other. She genuinely had feelings for me. She expressed to me that her not having night terrors while she was with me was just a refreshing perk. I was absolutely convinced she was being truthful with me.

I went on to express how much I liked her and saw a possible future for us. Her night terrors were nonexistent when she slept here, and knowing her true feelings toward me, she could hopefully use my place as a sanctuary, proven never she chose. It was an enormous house, and I would enjoy the company.

As we lay on the couch, I remember Jasmine squeezing me tight. We then closed our eyes, and we fell fast asleep.

Chapter Seven

It was ten in the morning by the time the aroma of the freshly brewed coffee in the basement was able to flood the entire house, which forced my eyes open. Jasmine was still asleep beside me. I was completely exhausted but knew this would be the most important day of my life.

I inched myself off the couch so as not to wake the snoring beauty. Before I went downstairs, I decided to shower—all the water beaded off my face quickly. I envisioned the possible future with Jasmine and me. There were children playing and scurrying about. Jasmine and I would be cuddled by the roaring fireplace as I read an article regarding my machine. They would discuss how the world would never be the same again due to my amazing work. My work had kept me busy for many years, and as a result, I never really had the opportunity to experience what life had to offer. But meeting Jasmine got me excited, and I now wanted to experience everything but with her.

After showering, I got dressed and threw on my lab coat. Jasmine's Chanel perfume lingered from the day before, making me smile. I decided before I went downstairs that I would wake her. She was going to have to sleep tonight for the experiment, and I wanted her to be good and tired. She resisted for a while but eventually sat up and stared at me. I prompted her to take a shower and to meet me downstairs. I pecked her cheek and let her be.

I was downstairs for a couple of hours before Jasmine came down. I assumed she fell back to sleep. I offered her coffee and asked if she wanted breakfast. She just laughed due to it being two in the afternoon. She exclaimed that she had found some fruit on the kitchen table and just helped herself. I poured Jasmine and myself a cup of coffee, and as we sipped, I asked if she had any thoughts about the experiment that I could clarify or answer any questions she may have had. Jasmine was nervous being in such an enclosed space and wanted to experience being inside the pod before the night approached. The feeling of being trapped in there still frightened her. She trusted me enough to ask if I could put her in. I admired Jasmine's courage. I handed her a two-piece bikini and directed her toward the change room. She hurried back, and by that time, I had already opened up the pod doors. Without hesitation, she walked up to the opening and climbed up the stairs, one foot at a time. Jasmine quickly encased herself. Everything about her was so mysterious. I thought she was initially afraid. In my profession, conjuring up the strength to attack obstacles when you're afraid is a power not many individuals harness. She was definitely a keeper in my book.

I walked up to the pod and peeked in. I watched as her eyes closed and her body bobbed up and down, trying to relax completely. Hypnotism was more effective when subjects were between awake and asleep, and her calm demeanor in the pod convinced me that the experiment would succeed.

"Are you ready?" I whispered.

Jasmine opened only one eye. "Oh, yes," she said in a soft meek voice.

"Okay," I uttered and walked toward the console. Without hesitation, I slammed down on the button, the door was closing, and I quickly got on to the intercom.

"Hello, Jasmine," I whispered. "I would be able to hear you at all times," I said and assured her she was doing well.

My voice must've reassured her, as Will's voice did to me because she rested for over forty minutes. And when I did let her out, the grin on her face was undeniable. She had fun in there, and she liked it.

The time was ticking down. Will was arriving at 6 pm. It was quarter past five, and my hunger was creeping up. With no time, I could not cook but recalled this Thai restaurant I ordered from. I decided to call, and with the whole group arriving tonight, I decided to make it a buffet. I would wine them, dine them, and then hypnotize them. That became our motto, by the way. As soon as those words left my lips, every test run after, like clockwork, one of us would utter that phrase.

Will arrived before the Thai food. I invited him to come to the basement and introduced him to Jasmine. After introductions, I asked Jasmine if she would be kind enough to mix up some drinks while Will and I headed to the garage to haul out an old wooden table and chairs I had stored just before I purchased the new ones, which were now sitting in my kitchen.

We lugged those dusty old antiques all the way from the garage to the basement. We positioned those atrocities, and just then, the doorbell chimed. I sprung to my feet and raced up the basement stairs. I opened the door, and I was surprised; it was Whoo-Lon standing there. He was the son of the owner of the Thai place. He had been delivering to me regularly up to six months ago. I remember a conversation we had; he was planning on opening up his own restaurant and was hoping I would try his menu, but I had not seen him since. When I asked him if he had succeeded, he began telling me that his mother had fallen ill, so he and his sister decided to take care of her while his father ran the Thai restaurant. Whoo was such a devoted son; I empathized with him. Whoo had orders to deliver and left. I paid him, gave him a very generous tip, and told him to take care.

As I closed the door, the food immediately caught my attention. One thing the family could do well was cook. Before I went down, I decided to call Samuel and Vanessa, hoping they could come earlier. Both were home, getting prepared, and had nothing else planned, so they were more than pleased to be invited. I explained that the food had just arrived and we were expecting them immediately. I hung up the phone and proceeded to the basement.

Will and Jasmine were sipping their drinks and getting acquainted. I explained to Will and Jasmine that I had called the rest of the group, and they were on their way. The drink Jasmine made me was waiting at the bar. I thanked her and kissed her cheek, then begged for another favor. I asked if she could help set everything out while I ran to get the plates and the utensils.

"My pleasure," she replied, pulling one of the bags toward her. By the time it took Jasmine and I to set up the table with the feast, the group had arrived. As Jasmine and I were putting on the finishing touches, the doorbell again chimed. Will, seeing we were occupied, offered to get the door. Vanessa was the first to arrive. I guess before Will could escort her downstairs, Samuel arrived because a second chime echoed through the house.

As the gang trotted to the basement, Samuel and Will were already chatting. It turns out that Will liked Samuel's 50s look and was commending him on it. I approached Samuel and thanked him for coming. Vanessa was quiet, standing in the background.

"Come in," I cried, directing her toward the table.

I began introducing everyone. Vanessa being the shy one, I decided to introduce her first. Will said hi first.

Samuel, again, did his kissing of the hand. Jasmine, being the fourth, introduced herself.

Having Jasmine there was important for Vanessa; she had more in common with her than us three old farts. Jasmine already knew Samuel from the last meeting, but I re-introduced them anyway. Samuel was polite; he just shook her hand this time, which showed me he was truly a gentleman and not a dirty old man.

We were delighted to finally be together. We all sat down at the table and enjoyed a wonderful meal. All I remember about that specific night, due to us having so many more like them, is that it was bonding. Those people sitting across this table from me were not just my patients; they would become so much more.

Chapter Eight

It turns ten pm. We had just finished dinner. I turned to Will and asked if he could fire up the chambers. A quiet hush filled the room. The mood quickly became tense. Will arose from his chair, picked up his napkin, and wiped his mouth. He then tossed the napkin into his empty plate, smacked his hands together, and screamed, let's do this. The group fled out this nervous chuckle. Will proceeded toward the council.

While he was setting up, I decided to clear the table. I gathered the dishes. Jasmine and Vanessa got up and opted to volunteer. The girls and I headed upstairs with the dishes. They were very helpful because they filled up the dishwasher while I put the leftovers away. While loading the dishwasher, I overheard the girls talking. I don't remember the specifics, but it involved her and some gay guy named Sven. They seemed to enjoy each other's company and were becoming friends. But we finished up in the kitchen and went back to the basement.

Samuel was hovering over Will at the controls, asking him about the drug I would be administering. When I approached, Will was trying to address Samuel's concerns; the girls were behind me. I took that opportunity to explain to them that the drugs were safe. Will then spoke up and reaffirmed my statement, which seemed to put everyone at ease.

The machine was humming and ready to go. Four bathing suits were laid out. I began first by removing my clothes—no sense in the group changing one at a time in the change room. In my opinion, it was wasted time. I completely disrobed and grabbed my bathing suit. Jasmine was the first one to follow, then Vanessa, and finally Samuel.

While the group changed, I asked Will to open the chamber doors. Changing in front of each other was not an issue. Darkness was now the only thing on our minds. We were set.

I asked if there were any last words before we proceeded. I am sure they had plenty, but nothing came to mind. I repeated if there were no questions, then each of them grabbed a pod. Vanessa and Jasmine took the two closest to the council. Samuel took the back left. That meant I got the back right.

One after the other, each of us entered. The water was still warm due to the constant flow of water running into the pods through a pressure hose. Even though we were in separate chambers, we were still connected by the constant flow of water and electricity. Will explained that there were intake and outtakes so the water wouldn't sit too long. The pod would always have the same amount of water but continuously fresh.

Pod doors closing, we heard bellow through the speakers. As the light vanished, I asked everyone if they could make out my voice. Simultaneously, the whole group answered yes. Everyone was calm and ready to go for phase two.

Will's voice poured through the speakers again. "Okay, gang, here we go. Here comes the juice."

As soon as he pressed the button to link us with the electricity, a huge cry came through the speakers. The group was feeling it. I knew it would be uncomfortable due to me experiencing the jolt already. The electricity ran through our bodies, and I reassured everyone that the initial feeling would pass quickly and they would soon adapt.

Five minutes had passed, and there was nothing but silence. Calmness filled the pods once again. I remember asking if they were good to go. It seemed like they forgot about the current surging through them because they were already in a soft voice.

I prompted them to close their eyes. I began talking about us bobbing up and down in the capsule. Up and down, up and down. I then told them to imagine they were sailing, bobbing up and down. Trying to imagine the wind cutting through their hair. I explained, hear the waves gently crash against the boat as you bob up and down. I repeated over and over as we sailed aimlessly on the dark blue sea. I told them to imagine darkness as we bob up and down, riding the waves of the sea. Up and down. Darkness engulfed us. I repeated, water still crashing against the ship—wind picking up. I uttered, "Up and down now, picture in the distance." I told them to imagine a light, extremely bright but tiny. I exclaimed, "We have to get to the light." I whispered, "Get to the light. Up and down, up and down."

Sailing closer and closer to the light. The waves heaved, and the light would disappear for a moment, then reappear. Then reappear, and disappear as we go up and down.

After about fifteen minutes, they were mine. At that moment, I prompted Will to inject the sleep inducer. Slowly, the needle punctured their necks. Due to them being in a hypnotic state, they felt nothing. Quietly, I lay in the chambers waiting for the drug to take effect.

As soon as the group reached REM sleep, Will informed me that everything was good to go. At that point, I attempted to contact out of the three of them; I thought I would be able to reach at least one.

Seven hours went by with no success. There were times when I screamed out, trying to reach them, but to no avail. As I lay in the dark, damp chamber, I remember all I could think was I failed them and what possibly could have gone wrong. I was at a loss, extremely tired. If I didn't leave the pod immediately I would have burst into tears. I had told Will to begin the reviving process, which consisted of turning up the electricity a fraction. The extra spark would take them out of REM sleep. At that point, I would count them down, starting from five all the way to one. The group woke up without any problems. Not one of them seemed to have experienced night terrors. In their opinion, the machine was working.

Not being terrorized while they slept was their objective, which was exactly what happened. My theory of being able to reach them was so far unsuccessful. The group and I exited the chambers all at the same time. We began drying ourselves off. It was 06:00 a.m. Will and I, being up all night, were completely exhausted. We need to sleep. As we dressed, Samuel and Vanessa began to discuss work and how it would be a different day due to them feeling refreshed. Jasmine wasn't as enthusiastic. She hated her job and was dreading going. She didn't say it, but you could tell by her reaction to Samuel's comment when he mentioned he loved flying and couldn't wait to get back to it. It looked to be quite overwhelming for her to know where she was going. Will was behind the council, packing up to go. He looked like I felt. When he looked up at the group, he caught me staring. We both knew the experiment didn't work, but he said nothing.

I decided to get the group's attention and explained I wanted a journal of everything they could remember while they slept. Write it down as soon as you can. I explained that's when dreams were the most vivid; I proceeded to escort them to the door. But when we got to the door, Jasmine decided to hang back. She just wanted me to know she had a really good time the other night and kissed me as she was leaving. She told me to call her later, and she left. I closed the door behind her and hustled to my room. I crawled into my king-size bed. My head hit the pillow, and I was gone.

Chapter Nine

During the next few months, the experiment, in my opinion, went without any success. We met three nights a week, but no contact was ever made. I was discouraged, to say the least. A cool side effect was that they were not being affected by their night terrors like before the experiment. The night terrors were still present, but the group seemed to be coping with them better than normal. Contact had not been achieved, but something was working.

Will and I discussed it in length and concluded that contacting the group while they hit REM sleep was no longer a priority as long as I could curb their fears. In my opinion, he was right, and the experiment was succeeding.

November rolled around. It was the 15th in the evening. I remember it vividly. I was staring out the kitchen window at the front street. It had been snowing all day. The streetlights were enhancing the flakes as they gently fell to the ground. How unique they were, I thought. Each one different from the other. When clumped together, you couldn't tell them apart. These people were quite similar. I thought individually we were quite unique, but bunched together, we were just a snowball.

As I peered through the window, I heard a faint clinking noise. I listened as it grew. Jasmine decided to come by. There she was, trudging through the snow in that atrocity of a vehicle. Whenever I heard that thing, it made me smile. Her noise-polluting car was just as good as any phone call.

She pulled up, and I was waiting for her at the door. I could feel the cold air attacking my bare feet. Jasmine got out of her car and proceeded up to the walk. Her hair was glistening from the fresh snow falling. Her smile filled the night sky. This woman had captured my heart.

She got to the door and greeted me with a soft kiss. She walked by me and playfully asked how I was doing. She referred to me that night as Sweetie, a nickname. I thought our relationship was blossoming but not ready for it. She appeared to be very happy. I knew the lack of night terrors had a lot to do with her attitude, and I was pleased with the experiment's effect on her.

I asked what I owed the pleasure to with her being there. She began to explain that she had just quit her job and she felt like celebrating. I had never celebrated when I lost a job before but to each its own. I knew how it was killing her anyway, and I was relieved to hear that she made the bold move. I was also interested in what she planned to do next. I asked what was in the cards for her near future. Jasmine wasn't worried. She continued to explain that her grandfather had just passed, and she was to inherit a couple of hundred thousand dollars.

"Bittersweet," she replied.

Knowing all her worries would soon be distant. Memories excited her. She loved her grandfather. He meant the world to her. But she also knew it was coming for some time.

"It was more of a blessing. Him passing," she uttered.

Due to him being bedridden for years, I wasn't sure how to react to the news. All I said was I felt sorry for her and, due to her grandfather's passing but continued to say that every cloud has a silver lining. I was pleased she gave up that thankless job. I recall acting so calm, but I think I was screaming inside. Jasmine was taken care of. She needed no help from anyone anymore. But she was still sitting here with me. I felt that at that moment, she truly loved me.

We snuggled on the couch watching some killer B movie about these perps trying to rob the jewelry store. The leader then caught one of his henchmen trying to conceal a precious gem worth millions. To make a long story short, the gem fell into a muddy swamp along with the gang leader as he caught a shot in the back by his partner's girlfriend and drowned.

Predictable plot and shabby acting made for a fun makeout session.

The movie finished. I asked Jasmine if she wanted more wine. She said yes and proceeded to follow me to the kitchen. How was the test going? She asked. I grabbed the wine from the crisper. Slow but steady, I replied, not really knowing what else to say. She then proceeded to ask why I wasn't reading their journals. Jasmine and the group had months of data written down and wanted me to analyze its content. She told me her dreams were becoming more vivid, but she felt unafraid. The journal was with her. It was peeking out of her purse, sitting on the counter while I poured the wine; she grabbed it.

I want you to read it, she said in a calm but demanding voice. This was the first time I saw that side of her boldness that got me wondering what she wrote. I gently snagged the book from her delicate fingers and picked up my wine glass and a half-empty bottle. Jasmine grabbed her glass, and we headed back to the living room. As we sat down, I felt Jasmine's eyes staring at her journal. I placed a wine bottle down on the table and slowly sat back with the book in one hand and my drink in the other. I looked at the book, motioning like I was about to read it. Playing around with her, I decided to take a sip of my wine instead. I felt her restlessness. Her body language was screaming for me to read the damn thing. I placed my drink on the table and held the book with both hands.

As I laid her writings on my lap, I began to stretch. She knew at that point I was fooling with her, so she gave me a strong right jab to the stomach and giggled.

"Stop it," she cried.

I let out a playful laugh and became very serious. I opened her journal and began reading. As I predicted, the first few pages were very difficult to comprehend. You could tell she was writing as soon as she woke. As soon as she walked about eight pages in, I came across Samuel's name. I began to giggle. She asked what was so funny. I then playfully accused her of having an affair with Samuel while she dreamt, she also let out a little giggle but then explained that she dreamt of him a lot. I told her it was due to association. She had been spending so much time with the group that it was only natural. I proceeded to read further. After another five pages, I realized she frequently dreamed of Samuel. I thought he must have reminded her of someone she trusted in her past, like her father, maybe her grandfather. She must have been substituting Samuel's face for theirs.

There was one paragraph in particular that caught my eye. She had mentioned people screaming. I remember Samuel having a similar dream like that. I just kept reading on. By the time I got down to the last few pages, she had begun talking about Vanessa. At that point, in Jasmine's dream, she remembers running through a forest alongside Vanessa. She recalled being chased by a snarling beast, but both of them were getting away. She wasn't worried, she wrote, due to both of them being together. I was intrigued.

Abruptly, I sprang out of my seat, still gripping Jasmine's journal. I raced to the phone and rapidly dialed Samuel's number. I remember his kid Josh answered. He was fifteen and very polite. Samuel was out at the time. I left a message saying to phone back as soon as possible. I then immediately phoned Vanessa. She was at home, giving herself a pedicure. I explained I needed her journal to go over. I wanted to charge her progress to see what her dreams entailed. Before letting her go, I asked if she remembered dreaming about anyone in the group. Vanessa became apprehensive at first.

"Why?" she exclaimed like trying to hide something.

I went on to explain that Jasmine had a dream that included her. During one of our earlier sessions, the dream Jasmine had resembled a dream Vanessa had told me about in confidence. Jasmine. Vanessa cried out, thinking back to her dream. Yeah. Jasmine, she went on. Coincidentally, she did have a dream concerning Jasmine.

As we went into the details, a chill shot down my spine. She repeated exactly what Jasmine had previously stated. She dreamt that she and Jasmine were running through the forest. They were being chased but remember getting away. Could this be possible? I thought. Could the group have been communicating all along?

I remember thinking I needed to speak to Samuel immediately. I needed to phone Will. I wanted to call the president. At that moment, I knew the only way I was going to truly know what was happening was to go under with them. I raced to rejoin Jasmine in the living room. I had so many questions for her. As we discussed her dreams in length, I was more convinced she had been communicating with the group while they slept. No wonder why they were coping so well with their night terrors. Without their knowledge. They seem to be helping each other, and I have not been there to guide them. If I was correct, the next session would be a memorable one. How right I was.

Chapter Ten

Samuel finally called me back the following morning. By the time he got home the night before, his son had already gone to bed. He explained the message was just given to him and he decided to phone. It was early. Samuel was getting his kids off to school and was hoping I was awake.

Due to the information I had received from Jasmine and Vanessa, sleeping was quite impossible. I felt overwhelmed with anticipation all night. Without any hesitation, I asked Samuel if any of his dreams involved Jasmine or Vanessa. Before he answered, I explained he was involved in both of theirs, and the similarities between dreams were too coincidental to miss. One of their dreams resembled a reoccurring night terror he and I discussed in line during our sessions.

When I first began informing him, Samuel became excited. He had been seeing both Vanessa and Jasmine but was embarrassed to bring it up. He then continued by telling me about a dream he had concerning Jasmine. The plane was in trouble just like before. He explained he was at the helm like always. When people began screaming and pleading, Samuel opened the cockpit door like he did every other time he had in this dream. When he cried out to the passengers, repeating he couldn't help, he set eyes on Jasmine. Jasmine was screaming along with everyone else. Jasmine recognized Samuel immediately and embraced him.

"What do we do?" Jasmine screamed.

Passengers were petrified. The plane was going down, and there was no one flying the plane. Samuel wanted nothing more than to save her, so he screamed at Jasmine to follow him quickly to the cockpit. They were going to land this plane themselves. Calm washed over Samuel which had given him courage. He didn't remember much more after that. This was becoming too real.

Our machine was a success. I was too eager to wait for our next session. I asked Samuel if he could come by that night. I was going under with them this time. Samuel was intrigued. It never crossed his mind that Jasmine was there with him while he dreamt. I let Samuel go and called Vanessa. I knew I was leaving a message because she worked the morning shifts. I was sure she would be more than excited to go under again, especially knowing what we now knew. After leaving a message, I decided to go wake Jasmine.

It just turned nine, and I smelled the coffee downstairs brewing. She and I made a ritual out of having coffee first thing while reading the paper. At this point, she had been spending most nights with me. Her place was becoming obsolete, and I was trying to conjure up the courage to ask her to let the house go and move in with me. Our relationship was running smooth, and asking her to change her lifestyle might shake things up. I was not sure if I was prepared for that. When Jasmine awoke, she had a long stretch. Her toes peaked out from under the covers from the end of the bed while her eyes slowly opened.

"Hey, baby," she uttered, still stretching. Jasmine smelled the nabob brewing downstairs. Coffee always got her up. I think she enjoyed our ritual just as much as I did.

After showering, we headed to the basement. As I brought us a cup of coffee, I told her we were having a session that night. I explained I was going to go under with them because I was convinced I would be able to make contact. I also stated that the dreams she was having concerning the group might actually be their dreams intersecting. She was not convinced, to say the least. We discussed her dreams in length that morning. She concluded that I might be reading too much into their dreams, seeing and hearing what I wanted to because I was so desperate to make contact. Being a psychologist, I had to agree that what she said was a possibility. The evidence, in my opinion, was enough, at least to beg the question. Whatever we said to each other that morning was irrelevant. I would know soon enough, and so would she.

The group was arriving around seven, and it was my turn to splurge for dinner. I had been running the test for about three months, and we had been taking turns buying. I remember this one time Vanessa ordered from this chicken place. Horrible food and extremely spicy. The gravy was watered down, and the chicken was dry. Thank goodness for alcohol because I don't think we cared after a couple of drinks. Food from that night seemed to linger with me, which prompted me to order from this new health place, the Herb Garden. Instead of meat, they use tofu; if you didn't know it was healthy food, you could not tell the difference. The only thing that was missing was the grease.

After coffee, I called Will and asked if he could come by. I wanted to fill him in on the situation and explain to him what had transpired within the last 24 hours. I gave him no specifics on the phone but informed him of a breakthrough I might have had. Will became extremely curious. He had a service call but decided to cancel and quickly come over.

Will arrived 20 minutes later. He headed to the basement and sat at the bar with Jasmine. I explained I had been reading Jasmine's journal and had also been in contact with Samuel and Vanessa. When I first pointed out the similarities in their journals, will seemed unimpressed. He didn't think that earlier, I thought to myself. Will then hypothesized that if the group somehow merged their dreams, their brainwaves would be consistent with each other.

With no warning, Will stood up and raced over to the council. He told us that every session we have had to date had been recorded. He brought up all of their brainwaves. Jasmine and I rushed to see what Will was up to. He had all of our brainwaves on separate monitors. At first, nothing seemed out of the ordinary. Will decided to fast forward due to hours of taping that needed to be watched. I had no idea what Will was searching for. I assumed he was trying to compare. I didn't think Jasmine knew what was happening either until Will slowed the tapes down.

"Do you see it?" he asked.

I saw nothing, but Jasmine exclaimed that she did. She explained that two of the four recordings looked identical to her and Samuel's. Will exclaimed that it was impossible, but it seemed to be happening nonetheless. He couldn't accept it at first. Will demanded it had to have been a mistake. He became possessed and began running through every piece of footage that was recorded tirelessly. He watched all morning and afternoon. Jasmine and I realized he was on a mission, left him alone, and decided to have a quickie in the shower.

After about an hour, I remember Jasmine and I were getting dressed when suddenly we heard Will scream from the basement. He found it again, two identical brainwaves. This time they were Jasmine and Vanessa's. He was convinced that something was occurring when they were sleeping. When I told Will I was going under with them this time, he was sure it would work. Will being as intelligent as he was concurring with my findings was more than enough to convince me contact was definitely going to happen this time. I knew it.

I decided to order pizza that night instead of healthy food. One thing I've learned in life is no matter how old you are; you can never go wrong with pizza. Plus, I knew it was a heavy meal and would tire us quickly.

My doorbell chimed at exactly seven. I knew it was Samuel. It was astonishing how punctual that man was. I can't recall one time since I've met the man where he was late, even by a minute. I swear, on some occasions, I thought he just stood outside and waited until the very second he was meant to arrive. Jasmine, being the sweetheart she was, ran upstairs to answer the door.

Later that night, she told me that when she got to the door to answer it, a party was waiting for her. Not only was Samuel there, but Vanessa was, and so was the pizza guy. I heard a burst of laughter bellowing from the kitchen that night and wondered what was so amusing. They were hollering close to five minutes before coming down. The laughter followed when the group arrived downstairs. Samuel was carrying the pizzas, with Jasmine and Vanessa following behind them. The ladies were giggling like two schoolgirls, and when I asked what the joke was, it just prompted them to laugh even harder. The whole situation was quite funny. Even Will, working over at the council, began laughing. It was a good icebreaker, to say the least. I never found out what the joke was.

The group and I sat around the table, scoffing down what I thought was the best pizza ever. It possibly could have been the joint Will lit up while we were eating. Jasmine and Vanessa had tried weed before. They were both the youngest of the group, so seeing them take a puff was not a big issue. But when I saw Samuel grab that joint, I was shocked. I remember letting out one of those geeky screams again, which scared the hell out of them. Everyone just sat there silent until they realized why I yelled and howled. I have to admit, seeing Samuel stoned was quite amusing. He wasn't doing anything different; he just did it slower. Will really got a kick out of Samuel. I don't know how many times Will hugged him and told Samuel he liked him, but I found it to be very entertaining. We were intoxicated that night. I considered holding off the experiment till the following day, but my eagerness prevented it.

It was eleven that night when we decided to turn on the machine. I was so intoxicated. I don't even remember staggering into the chamber. I remember that was the night I had the most vivid dream I had ever experienced. I was swimming in the ocean. Darkness filled the sky. I could feel waves crashing into my face, making breathing difficult. My goodness, it was so real. I recall feeling like I was going to drown. And there was nothing I could do.

As I tirelessly treaded water, I felt something brush up against my leg. When I felt it for the second time, I was prompted to swim. A feeling of terror crept up as I began to swim faster. I swam so fast, I remember, and for such a long time. I wasn't fast enough, though. No matter what I tried, I could not rid myself of this unidentified object. I swam for what seemed like an eternity, and just when I thought I lost it, I felt a tentacle wrap around my leg and attempt to pull me under. I fought this fierce creature with every ounce of fight I had left, but the tentacle overpowered me. It was latched onto my whole leg and was tightening its grip. I was being pulled under.

The last thing I recall was envisioning Vanessa. I had no idea why, but it saved my life. A moment had passed, and I opened my eyes to see that I was no longer in the ocean. It had disappeared, and I found myself standing in the middle of what looked like a jungle. It was so authentic. The heat was wretched, the air damp, and the mosquitoes were eating me alive. Glancing around within minutes, I realized that I was dreaming. It was the sun that tipped me off. I wonder where it came from when it was utter darkness not more than two minutes ago. The more I thought it through, the clearer it became.

At one point, I remembered actually recalled being in the chamber at homeland, remembering I was to search for the group. That's when I heard it.

Chapter Eleven

I began searching for the group. A disturbing howl poured through the forest. I swiftly dove, ducking behind the first tree I glanced upon. I wasn't sure what the sound was or where it came from, but I assumed it to be quite ferocious.

I recall feeling naked and vulnerable sitting out in the open. So in a panic, I peered around, searching for the perfect hiding place. Glancing around, determining which way to sprint, I discovered a group of bushes to my left, not more than 50 yards away. I didn't want to move away from the tree shielding me. I felt absolutely petrified, but clenched my fists together, stood up, and sprinted toward the bushels. I was halfway to my new hiding spot when the fearsome roar returned. Immediately, my heart felt like it was beating out of my chest. I was horrified, but my legs refused to stop.

As I got to the bushes where I intended to hide, my name echoed through the leaves. The voice I heard was familiar and stopped me in my tracks. I stood there, listening to the voice bellowing through the forest. It was female and getting closer. I rapidly scoped out the forest, screaming, "Hello, anyone there? Hello?"

Ahead in the distance, I noticed movement coming from the shadows, and again I cried, "Hello?"

As the shadow grew closer, Vanessa appeared. I screamed her name to make sure I had her attention. When she peered ahead and saw me with a gigantic smile, she looked very happy to see me. She darted toward me with her arms, ready for me to embrace her. Being just as ecstatic to see a familiar face, I began racing toward her.

The terror in her eyes was visible to me and growing, and I knew she needed me to calm her. Vanessa was racing toward me as fast as she could, then, without notice, tripped over a rock that had no business being there. Vanessa went down hard.

At that moment, the mysterious roar flooded the forest again. I stopped running for a second, frantically scoping out my surroundings. Whatever was out there seemed to have gained on us and sounded closer than ever. Vanessa appeared to be okay because she stood up and began sprinting again toward me.

This wild, unknown creature continued to roar with me, roaring right back. I pleaded with Vanessa to hurry. She immediately caught up, threw her arms around my neck, and hugged me. Still hugging, I began dragging her running back toward the bushes I intended to hide it before I heard her. While running, I asked if she was hurt after taking that terrific tumble. I knew Vanessa to be a strong-willed individual. Since our first encounter, I have seen nothing truly affect her except her night terrors. So when I asked her that, I knew she was fine.

Her dreams genuinely terrified her. So, in this case, Vanessa's inability to sleep after what I experienced firsthand seemed to be warranted. Other than being scared, Vanessa was fine. She then asked if I was okay, but before I could answer, she wanted to know what the hell I was doing in the middle of the jungle.

"Good question," I replied. But just before I could answer, a rustling noise came behind us, drawing our attention. We peered back to pinpoint the noise when three enormous snarling wolves were already charging toward us. We both screamed for our lives, but abruptly I clamped on to Vanessa's hand and began to race toward the bushes. Violent roars echoed behind us as we scurried. We both knew they were gaining on us, but all we could do was run. Still holding Vanessa's hand, we reached the bushes and leaped over them, hoping it would hide us and possibly confuse the violent animals. Soaring through the air. I caught myself thinking of Samuel, perhaps because Vanessa and I were flying through the air, and it made me think of planes, which was consistent with Samuel's profession, and instantaneously Vanessa and I both were now on this plane, surrounded by screaming, hysterical passengers. Vanessa never once let my hand go. I, with great effort, began focusing on the plane's surroundings but was experiencing a little dizziness from just being chased by rabid dogs and now trying to comprehend how we ended up on the plane. Looking around, I realized that everyone was panicked because the plane seemed to be out of control and going down.

Vanessa and I realized that we were still in danger and began pushing people out of the way. I had a suspicion, and to prove it right, I needed to get to that cockpit. While we raced toward the front of the plane, Vanessa asked what the hell we were doing. I explained to her that if I was correct, Samuel would be on the other side of this door flying this plane. She didn't understand at first why Samuel would be flying the plane. I found it absolutely fascinating. Vanessa didn't realize we were dreaming.

We reached the cockpit door, and both of us began to bang. Pounding, I explained to Vanessa that we were still in the chambers at my house. At first, she didn't believe me. She exclaimed. I was absurd. We called Samuel's name to open the door; all the while, she insisted I was crazy and that I needed to see a psychiatrist myself. I laughed at this because that would have been pretty ironic. Screaming flooded the cockpit. Samuel pleaded with us to leave him alone because he couldn't help. I continued to rap on the door, demanding him to let us in. Recognizing Samuel's voice, Vanessa joined in again, screaming that it was her and me at the door. I looked at Vanessa and smiled because I knew she was convinced. We stared into each other's eyes for a second, then continued to bang the plane.

At this point, the plane abruptly took a nosedive. We were going down quickly as the pressure in the cabin pushed Vanessa and me against the cockpit door. Just at that moment, when neither of us couldn't take it anymore, the lock turned. Samuel was coming out, the door opened, and Vanessa and I fell backward into the cockpit. Samuel screamed at us to leave him alone. He wasn't able to help us. I grabbed Samuel by his jacket and pleaded with him to look at my face.

"Who am I, Samuel?" I yelled when he looked up. It took him a second, but he soon recognized both of us. He was confused as to why we were on this particular flight. I screamed for him not to worry about why we were here and get back to the controls and fly the damn plane. I knew we were dreaming, but it was so vivid. I literally had to remind myself several times that I was dreaming just to keep from checking out again.

Samuel attempted to get control of the plane, but I was struggling. I wasn't sure what to do, but sitting in the copilot's chair while Samuel was flying a plane without a copilot concerned me greatly. But I felt we had more pressing issues to deal with. Samuel and I tried to land the plane, and I took that moment to attempt to explain to Samuel that he was in the dream.

"Try and remember," I asked. "Remember where we were before getting on the plane. Remember where you were before getting on the plane," I said. He couldn't recall. At first, the pressure he was under flying the plane prevented him from concentrating on anything else. Vanessa was standing behind us, sweating and screaming because we were moments away from hitting the ground at an accelerated speed. I told her to stop freaking out and help me. Seeing Samuel in the cockpit, as I said, we would convince her fully.

She told me later in one of our sessions that she actually even remembered being asleep in the chamber.

Vanessa put her hand on Samuel's shoulder and reassured him this was a dream. She continued by telling him we were still asleep in the deprivation chambers. She asked if Samuel remembered Jasmine and us needing to find her. Samuel, at that point still clouded, slowly put it all together. He repeated Jasmine's name, then asked where she was. It didn't even dawn on me until that exact minute Jasmine wasn't there. I demanded we land the plane immediately and find her. Talking about Jasmine made us forget we were in dire jeopardy and falling to our doom. I believe it was because we all thought of her at that moment. That was the key.

We had seconds before we hit the ground. I grabbed Samuel and Vanessa's hands, pulled them close, and told them to picture Jasmine. We all quickly closed our eyes, frantically trying to picture Jasmine's face while bracing for impact as the plane plummeted toward the earth. Everything abruptly went silent. Reluctantly, I opened my eyes and found we were no longer on the plane but in an elevator. Vanessa and Samuel were still bracing for impact beside me. When I recommended they open their eyes, I reassured them they were safe. The crouching tigers opened their eyes, and for a moment, being in the elevator clouded their thinking. They once again forgot they were dreaming. I actually had to remind them several times. I actually had to explain how imperative it was to remind each other constantly. It was very easy to get sidetracked, I told them.

The elevator stopped on the third floor. The door slid open, and Jasmine was standing right there, waiting to get on the elevator. We stared right at each other. I smiled from ear to ear. She just looked away, like she didn't even recognize me. We were all there puzzled. Jasmine was standing at the front of the elevator, with her back towards us now. I look at Samuel and Vanessa, wondering what I should do. Vanessa motioned with her head for me to get Jasmine's attention. So like the geek I was, I coughed, hoping she would turn around but was unsuccessful. Vanessa then motioned again, saying that I was pathetic, and then attempted to get Jasmine's attention on her own. She leaned over and tapped Jasmine on the shoulder. Jasmine spun around and saw us standing there, surprising the crap out of her. She had no idea why we were there in the building and asked who we were meeting with. Jasmine had no idea we were dreaming either. I found it fascinating and how difficult it was to convince them. It was like something was trying to prevent us from remembering.

When we all tried to explain to Jasmine that we were all in a dream state, she thought we were completely nuts. When we persisted, she became irritated and began to tell us she was there for a job interview and didn't need us screwing it up for her. She was adamant, but I just couldn't back down. I continued trying to convince her. I reminded her of the waitress job that she recently quit and the experiment we were running. Still unsure, I began to predict what would happen when the elevator doors opened. I felt if I predicted what was about to occur, I'd have her totally convinced.

We all stood there in silence, waiting for my prediction to come true. The elevator doors finally slid open. Nothing was out of the ordinary. The floor looked like every other floor. Jasmine was pissed and glared at me. She said that she found none of this amusing and that we should just go home. I explained that something was wrong and the floor shouldn't have been there. Even when I heard myself utter that sentence for a second, I thought I might have been crazy.

Jasmine stepped out of the elevator, and I quickly followed, with Samuel and Vanessa trailing right behind. She knew we were following and was already irritated. She took not more than three steps and turned around, intending to scream or hit me or something, but when she spun around, she just stood there in complete silence. All she did was stare. Being curious. Samuel, Vanessa, and I quickly turned back to see what Jasmine was looking at. When we spun around, we found ourselves staring at this gigantic white wall, which we all knew was once an elevator. What the hell is going on? Samuel cried out. Jasmine had no idea either. She just stood there, staring in silence.

At that moment, I reminded all of them once again that they were dreaming. Jasmine just couldn't believe it. She couldn't grasp it. I think she was in denial. Until we all turned around again. We saw exactly what Jasmine saw in her dreams — a winding road where the building should have been. No more hallways, no more doors, no more convincing was needed. I began to explain that we were here solely to control these terrifying adventures. Nothing in here could actually hurt us. I probably shouldn't have said that because the trail began to crumble from behind us no sooner than I spoke. Jasmine screamed for us to run. Without hesitation, we all began to sprint down this unknown trail, trying to outrun the inevitable.

The nightmare was unfolding, just like Jasmine described during our sessions. Nothing happening to us was real, but it still felt real, and it compelled us to run. The inevitability of this nightmare was that we fell to the ground, and it seemed like we were extremely high. I knew I didn't have much time. I thought that if this was a dream, we had to have had some control.

Racing down the path I pleaded with the group to picture the chambers. "Remember that we were sleeping down in the basement?" I exclaimed.

The moment we began envisioning ourselves bobbing up and down in those dark cylindrical pods, I was able to begin to count us down backward from five. I told the group when I got to four; I already had flashes of being inside the pod. By the time I got to two, I felt the sensation reverse itself. I was experiencing flashes of the dream but was now safely in the pod. When I finally counted us down, I was completely coherent.

I called through the speakers to see if everyone was fine. They were all awake and accounted for. Our first trip was a complete success.

Will's voice screamed through the speakers. "That was fucking awesome; you guys."

While Will monitored our progress through the entire night, he began to explain that he knew the moment we were in contact with each other.

The most exciting part of the night, Will said, is when all four of our brainwaves synchronized. He couldn't believe we all found each other. But he was puzzled about how we revived ourselves because there was still an hour before he was to wake us up. I explained that after some convincing on my part and lots of concentration, we became very aware of our surroundings and where we were. Then all we had to do was concentrate on picturing ourselves in the chambers. I counted them down, I told him. That's all it took. I explained that I could bring them back as long as I was present. Will was supposed to increase the electricity to wake the group. I needed them semi-awake, so I could count them down. But due to my presence, that was no longer needed. It was probably for the best because I knew how dangerous it was to introduce electricity to water.

I wanted everyone to get their journals and write down everything they could recall. I advised them that I would also start a journal so we could all understand what was truly going on and compare notes.

The group got dressed, sat at the table, and everything was silent for an hour. We wrote down every wonderful adventure we had just experienced. Will finished shutting off the machine and wiped down the chambers. Then prematurely turned on the coffee maker. He assumed we could all use a cup, and he was right. He did everything. Even brought our cups and set them down on the table. I think he was pretty excited. He had been up all night, but you couldn't tell. I think we were all feeling quite elated to be able to make contact that we did and still remember it when we woke. I think it would be overwhelming for anyone.

One by one, we finished our journals and placed them on the table. I think we were all still in our own heads going over that night because everyone was dead quiet. We sat around just sitting in our coffee, staring into space.

I decided to discuss what transpired because the signs began making me uneasy. I began explaining that we were at the beginning of what was finally going to be ridding ourselves of these night terrors. The group seemed to like the sound of that. I continued by explaining what we had just experienced. That night was open to manipulation, which meant as soon as we became experienced enough, I believe we could control these dreams instead of them controlling us.

Vanessa needed to get home and asked Samuel if he could give her a lift with the kids off to school, which was very convenient. Will also wanted to leave. He needed some sleep. He had been up all night, and I think it was now catching up to him. The gang said their goodbyes and departed. Jasmine had no obligations that day and asked if she could hang back. She never wanted me to feel like she was taking advantage, so she always asked to stay. Everything about Jasmine made me smile. You know, I knew she was the one for me. I was just hoping that she felt the same.

I decided I wasn't waiting anymore. I was going to ask her to move in with me.

Chapter Twelve

Jasmine and I were lying in bed. I recall tickling and blowing on her stomach. She laughed hysterically and slapped me on the back, telling me to quit. But whenever it looked like I was about to, she would poke my ribs to agitate me further. Jabbed to my ribs was where it was sensitive, which compelled me to jump up and get on top of her. Pinning her shoulders down with my knees and playfully, I began tapping her face with my fingertips. Attempting to free herself, Jasmine began to fight back, but she knew she couldn't overpower me. She let out a defeated laugh. I then took my knees off of her arms and lay beside her. We gazed into each other's eyes. I slowly pulled her close to me, and I remember kissing her so passionately, then gently pulled her lips away, still gazing. I had no more doubts. I decided that would be the moment I would ask her to move in with me.

I began by asking her how she felt about me. I was nervous, too, I remember, because this type of conversation could make or break a relationship. When I finally gained the courage to ask, she answered yes immediately. I almost recall sobbing. She said she had been waiting for me to ask. She then continued to express her undying love for me and how truly happy she was. Her mood then changed as she became apprehensive. She began to explain the very same concerns that she had with this relationship she had with her previous relationships. When I told her what I thought and how relationships were always a gamble, she completely agreed. Her skepticism stemmed from her previous relationships with that creep she and I discussed in detail. After she realized her concerns were unfounded, she again agreed to move in. She explained that she knew I was nothing like her ex and was just terrified to lose me. I reassured her I wasn't going anywhere and was absolutely in love with everything about her. She then expressed her love for me again and began to cry. I realized it was a huge step, and she was regressing to the incident with her last boyfriend. So for the rest of the night, I just held her close until we both fell fast asleep.

A couple of days went by without contact with the group. We were supposed to go under again that night, and I felt ready as ever; I recall Jasmine was excited as well. It was incredible how well she was sleeping. The nightmare was present. She told me she was just able to feel better. She explained when she was engulfed in her night terror; there were points she remembered she was dreaming. It calmed her greatly. My advice to her when we went under initially stuck in her subconscious, and she was able to utilize it. I was impressed.

The machine, in my opinion, was working better than expected. For her to realize she was dreaming without any supervision was miraculous. I was hoping the other group members were having just as much success.

It was still early, and my subjects wouldn't arrive until later. I decided Jasmine, and I would go ice skating down at the river. The trails that were built went on for miles. Jasmine told me she used to go there with her family, so I thought it would be a very nice surprise. I even bought her a pair of skates and gave them to her in the car when we arrived.

The whole day was absolutely magical. The continuous smile on her face melted my heart. I played organized ice hockey right through to high school when I was a teenager. So before we got to the rink, I considered myself a pretty decent skater until I saw her move. She was so graceful and elegant. Her ability on those skates exuded great talent and tireless practice. When I asked where she learned, she explained it was because of her father. He had such high hopes for her and strived to get her into the Olympics. After years of practice, Jasmine added that skating wasn't important anymore and quit. When she told her dad, they got into a huge argument, and she moved out. She explained she quit because of that creep she thought loved her. She thought she would spend the rest of her life with him, but she got blindsided when she found him cheating. Jasmine felt like such an idiot for quitting ice skating. On so many occasions, she wanted to speak with her father but felt embarrassed. Everything started to make sense. I now understood why she was waitressing when she absolutely dreaded it. She was proving she could take care of herself. She wanted to show her father. The ego is a funny thing. In my opinion, the situations we put ourselves to save face and prevent ourselves from having to say we screwed up is God's joke on us to give us youth before wisdom.

Jasmine was so quick on her skates before we arrived I thought I would take it easy on her. The little firecracker had to slow down for me. There were times she even made fun of me, circling me over and over. I guess it was amusing, depending on what side you were on. I was panting, for goodness sake. Jasmine wasn't even breathing heavy. She just laughed. That's when I decided to tackle her into the snow and then give her a good face wash. We both lay there giggling as I wiped away the snow from her face and jacket. She suddenly just up and kissed me. This kiss felt different. I don't know how, but it was. I think what I felt was love that day.

After the moment passed, we lay in the snow drinking the hot chocolate I had made just for this occasion. As we sat in the freezing snow, inevitably, a chill crept up on us, so we quickly finished and headed home. Jasmine and I arrived back home around five. I didn't tell her, but she wiped me out. I think the little show-off knew it too but didn't say anything. She probably thought I would never skate with her again, which did cross my mind once or twice. She was so fast. Her being as talented as she was, was well deserved. To be that talented at something takes a lot of dedication. And after the muscles stopped screaming, I concluded that she was entitled to show off a little. Jasmine sprinted to the living room.

Dr. Phil was on, and she was mesmerized by this bald dude. I think she had a fascination with psychologists. While she engulfed herself on TV, I decided to take a shower. I was hoping the hot water would ease my throbbing pain.

While I let the water saturate my hair, I began feeling faint. I literally had to drape myself against a wall to stop myself from falling. I recall shaking my head a couple of times, trying to fight it off, focusing on my breathing, when everything suddenly went dark for a few seconds, the water beaded on my head while the feelings slowly began to pass. I felt tired from overexerting myself, so I decided to finish my shower and crawl into bed. I needed a couple of hours to rejuvenate myself before everyone arrived in the evening.

When I woke up, I remember the blanket my mother had knitted for me for Christmas was draped over my body. Jasmine, being the angel, grabbed it out of the linen closet and covered me up. She was curled up behind me, sleeping with her arm hanging over me. Everything she did elate me. I had never spent much time with people due to my working in a school; plus, I was convinced it was better that way, so I was not to be distracted. Meeting Jasmine, Will, and the rest of the group made me wonder if I might have missed out because they were such amazing people.

I recall it was a quarter past eight when I checked the clock. With Jasmine's arm wrapped around me, I began to caress her shoulder, asking her to wake up lightly. I shuffled my body around to face her and gently caressed her nose with mine. Jasmine's eyes crept open for a moment just to acknowledge me, and then she slowly closed them again. I didn't have the heart to wake her. She must have been tired as well from skating all day, so I kissed her on the forehead and left her alone.

Will arrived close to nine. He always liked to get to my place early to check out the machine and have a few drinks with me. Since Jasmine and I met, Will and I weren't spending much time together. I knew he was alone with his dog and felt bad for him most of the time. Face it; there is only so much you can say to your dog before you start feeling like you're talking to yourself. Letting him come over to chill with me was therapeutic. He needed human interaction, and I needed a techie—two birds with one stone in my book.

Will and I were downstairs sipping whiskey and shooting a game of pool. He had nothing on me. That table and I had been together for seven years. I knew every slant, curve, and blemish on her. My father and I built it from scratch in the garage. My father never admitted it, but I knew it was his way of spending time with me. It took a whole year to build that baby, and during that time, I moved out and acquired this place. When we finished building the table, my father asked how I intended to move it. He was giving it to me as a housewarming present. At first, I told him I couldn't possibly take it due to all the work we had put into it, but what my dad told me at that point would stick with me for the rest of my life. My dad was not a sensitive guy in the slightest, so to hear him speak as he did, you can imagine my surprise. He began telling me the pool table was always going to be mine. He wanted me to have something that reminded me of him because he knew I was graduating that year, and I wanted to get my own place. He continued by telling me that buying a pool table was easy, but building one created more than a game. It built memories that I could remember forever. I tried to be strong when he said that, but it was the nicest thing he had ever said to me that I began to cry. He hugged me that day. My dad did not hug me since I was twelve years old. We loved each other. He just wasn't good with emotion. I think that was a big part of why I became a psychologist.

The doorbell chimed. It was nine, right on the nose. Will and I both knew Samuel's punctuality, so when we looked at the clock, we laughed. It never failed. I was just about to run upstairs and answer the door when I heard Jasmine running to get it. Will only had one ball left on the table, plus the eight ball. I remembered him saying that I was not getting off that easy, then took his shot, but missed. Knowing the group had just arrived, I decided to show Will how it was done. Up to this point, I had been taking it easy on him only because he was terrible at the game. I still had four balls left on the table, plus the eight ball, and without any notice quickly sharpened them. I sunk them fast, caught a glimpse of his jaw-dropping out of the corner of my eye while ball after ball vanished, and when I called the eight ball bankside and made it, he was absolutely disgusted. Will threw his arms up in the air and told me to go screw myself. I just laughed. Will, being the stand-up guy he was, walked over to me and shook my hand. He realized I took it easy on him and thanked me. Sharking him all night would have been entertaining, he said, chuckling. Playing pool, you learn to stay humble due to the fickleness of the game. I explained and told him not to sweat it. I felt a pep talk was warranted, but I might have embarrassed him a little by cleaning up so quickly.

The basement door opened, and everyone came charging down like a herd of elephants. Vanessa arrived with Samuel because they both lived very close to each other and found it more convenient. Also, it was Vanessa's turn to spring for dinner, and instead of ordering out, Vanessa decided to cook this unbelievable lasagna. I swear I have never tasted anything that good in my life. With every bite we took, it was just getting better and better. We couldn't stop complimenting her; it was so divine, and at this point, I think we began to embarrass her. Vanessa was very humble as well and had trouble with receiving compliments. Her face became cherry red after a while, but we couldn't help it. The dish was magnificent. Vanessa studied culinary art. She exuded such skill. The owner of the Monsieur Bistro hired her as soon as she graduated. Vanessa's mentor gave her a good word because he knew she was a natural and learned quickly. It was a good call, too, because she became the head chef within a year. To make a long story short, we ate the whole lasagna.

Will and Jasmine were still picking out of the pan when I realized it was getting close to eleven. I was eager to take a ride in the silver shuttle. I prompted Will to stop picking food out of the pan, and told him to warm up the machine. We all chuckled, and comically Jasmine grabbed the pan, pulled it close, and shielded it with her arms. Mine, she exclaimed, continuing with the joke. Will began pulling at the pan she was guarding so heavily, playing tug of war just for a minute before he finally relinquished it to go turn on the machine.

The group and I changed into our suits and stood in front of our designated chambers. We all felt different; this time, we had no fear at all. Quite the contrary, we felt the feeling of control this time. The pod doors opened as I started inside. I recalled thinking that another world was awaiting our arrival. Where were we going to wake up next? Before we entered, I encouraged the group to keep each other in their thoughts. The last time we went under, we were drawn to Jasmine because we focused on her. If my hypothesis was accurate, we would find each other that much easier. The group agreed. Jokingly, Samuel said he was thinking of Jasmine and Vanessa already. I found his comments to be quite funny but a little perverse.

He entered the pod, still laughing at what Samuel said. You could hear the girls giggling, probably due to them feeling flattered by the comment. We submerged our bodies and relaxed ourselves. The laughter subsided, and they became silent. Will's voice bellowed through the speakers, telling us to get ready, and the doors began to close. Even though I had experienced the ride already, my heart was still racing. Will then warned us that the electricity was on its way. This was always amusing for Will. It never failed. We would all scream when the surge reached our bodies, followed by a muffled giggle from Will. The feeling dissipated quickly, and we relaxed again.

The group was prepped before I began hypnosis. I reminded them once again to keep each other in their thoughts.

"Focus on the chambers," I uttered, beginning to put them under. "Here we go," I said. "Up and down. We go up and down. Feel the water around your bodies bobbing up and down," I reiterated. "Now imagine we are on a ship together," I continued. "Feel the waves crashing into the sides of the boat, causing water to leap off, splashing us. Now picture a light," I told them. "Extremely tiny but very significant. Get to that light," I exclaimed. "As we go up and down. Up and down."

Once I had the group under, Will injected the sleep-inducer. Only seconds had passed. I had already felt the drug coursing through my veins. That was all I could recall. I was out.

Chapter Thirteen

This dream began precisely the way it did the first time. My fear of the water apparently had no place to hide. At that moment, terror crept up on me. I recalled the unidentified sea creature I encountered last time and was now anticipating its arrival. Searching for the group was still at the forefront of my mind. Feeling panicked, I called out the first name that came to me—Samuel. I cried, knowing he would be my best bet for survival.

Suddenly, bubbles appeared, coming up from the water. I immediately became petrified, not able to move a muscle. The creature was back and was about to pull me under again. The bubbles grew larger as my nemesis quickly surfaced to the top. Instead of the monster I expected to appear from beneath me shooting up from the water, it was Samuel. When he first sprang from the water, I screamed in escalation. We quickly paddled toward each other, laughing and yelling in astonishment. We clasped our hands together, pulling each other close, and gave each other a manly embrace. We were tirelessly dreading water.

When I asked Samuel how he found me, he explained he had no idea. He remembered being on the plane where they were in trouble like always, but this time he was aware of it being a dream. He continued explaining how he screamed for us, but help never arrived. I was curious as to why I wasn't pulled into his subconsciousness like I pulled him into mine. Samuel went on, explaining that right before the plane hit the ground, in his night terror, he appeared underwater, frantically having to swim to the top for air. And there I was. Samuel then asked if I had seen the girls. Sarcastically I responded, no, not yet. I then added, chuckling that I had been a tad busy treading water and fearing for my life. Samuel abruptly broke into laughter, which prompted me to laugh even louder, which made Samuel laugh even harder.

So there we were, shredding water in the middle of the ocean, with the real possibility of being pulled under at any moment, and we were laughing in hysteria. Moments passed, and we both calmed ourselves. As it became quiet, I suggested that we probably should begin looking for the others. I encourage Samuel to think about Jasmine. I was confident that if we both pictured her face, one of two things would occur; all three of us would be treading water, or we would propel ourselves into her dreams—just treading water. Samuel and I focused on Jasmine.

Within seconds, we found ourselves out of the water, going dry, and standing in a bedroom consumed with pink paraphernalia. I swear it was draped over everything. At first, Samuel and I thought we might be in the wrong place because nobody was in the room, and nothing seemed familiar to us. Plus, I absolutely despise this colored pink. I proceeded to the bedroom door to see where it led when a picture taped to a mirror hanging on the wall drew my attention. The first thing that caught my eye was the dreadful pink frame. I found it quite atrocious. When my eyes focused on the photo of the picture, it was identical to Jasmine when she was a child. One thing Jasmine liked to do more than anything was to take pictures. Many nights I was forced to view her albums, pretending to be interested. Not to sound cruel, but she took a lot of snapshots. She took pride in her pictures. She went as far as to date every picture and added little quotes, plus who was in the pictures. I have to admit I was impressed at the work she put into them. When she first brought one out to view, I was intrigued to learn about her life. What I was not aware of was she had over 40 more of them, completely full and still growing.

As soon as I saw the picture taped to the mirror, I knew we were in the right place. I told Samuel that I recognized Jasmine in the picture, and I was convinced she had to be there somewhere. And one thing that was puzzling me was why we ended up in Jasmine's Pepto Bismol palace. Samuel liked that one. Something drew us there. Samuel suggested that if we waited around, she might just show up, hoping he was right. We waited for a while and decided to scan the place for clues.

While looking around, I noticed Barbie dolls lined up on this long wooden dresser. Also, tons of stuffed animals had been neatly placed on the bed. I knew the room was inhabited by a younger girl, not a woman like Jasmine. I voiced my concerns to Samuel. Him being a father, I valued his opinion. He assured me I was right. We asked each other, why would we be drawn to this room in particular if Jasmine wasn't there? Waiting got me thinking aloud. "If the dream was when Jasmine was a child," I stated to Samuel, "maybe it was a night terror where she was in trouble with her parents, and she would storm through the door at any second."

Samuel and I, already staring at each other, both simultaneously turned our attention to the door, waiting for her to walk in. A couple of seconds lapsed as we watched, hoping she would, when we both stared back at each other we began to laugh.

"I guess not," Samuel replied.

We just couldn't figure out what the room had to do with Jasmine, other than it being her room as a child. Samuel suggested we try focusing on her again, possibly taking us somewhere different. Nothing indicated she would ever arrive, so I agreed because it was the best idea we had.

Just as we attempted to contact Jasmine once again, I scanned around the room one last time when I noticed there were no pillows on the deck. It got me thinking because everything in the dream was relevant. No pillows. She had to have owned at least one. I thought if I were a child, where would I take my pillows? I wondered what? At that very moment, I had an epiphany. I dropped to my knees and peered under the bed. There, curled up in a ball, was Jasmine sleeping on her pink pillows. Jasmine must have conjured this memory up because it was pleasant for her, not a night terror at all. My only concern was if she would recognize in that particular reality she might have aped the mentality of a child. I gently nudged her shoulder with my hand and asked her to wake up. At first, she didn't respond, so I nudged her harder, whispering that it was me. Jasmine opened her eyes and recognized my voice. Immediately she felt groggy and was unsure where she was. She quickly sprang up, hitting her head on the roof of her bed, and went crashing to the floor again. While she lay there rubbing her goose egg, she asked where she was. I told her we were in what looked like her room when she was a child, she was absolutely befuddled—crawling out from under the bed. She asked why we were all there in her room she hadn't seen for close to 15 years. She was completely oblivious to the fact that we were dreaming. Samuel and I had to sit her down to convince her for what felt like way over an hour.

It was fascinating how these realities played with our minds. Jasmine came around and remembered everything. She even realized Vanessa wasn't there and knew we needed to find her. She was so coherent; she even wanted to lead this time; she was ready to leap to the next reality and disturb some dreams.

We all latched onto each other's hands and focused on Vanessa. The sensation this time felt very different. I experienced complete darkness this time, which lasted close to five minutes. Usually, crossover from dream to dream felt instantaneous. But that particular time dragged and without notice we found ourselves engulfed in blinding daylight. Jasmine, Samuel, and I were still together, sitting amongst complete strangers on the grass in a park. We were grouped up in a circle, with Samuel sitting to the left of Jasmine and me on the right. The people we sat with were enjoying an afternoon picnic and didn't seem to notice us at all. Not one person in the group even remotely resembled Vanessa. But from our previous situation with Jasmine, I knew she would be lurking somewhere.

I stood up and began to scope around the park in hopes she was somewhere close. I peered all around, even in the trees, but with no luck. I walked back towards Jasmine and quietly whispered into her ear, asking if she saw any indication of Vanessa. She saw nothing, and Samuel remarked she's always been a little nutty.

A moment later, a shadow appeared from behind us, blocking up the sun, when a voice sarcastically uttered, "Yeah, well, at least I'm not old."

The three of us abruptly turned back in anticipation, knowing we would see Vanessa hovering over us.

"What took you guys so long?" she exclaimed.

Samuel foolishly responded by saying we couldn't find a taxi, which got no response at all. Vanessa was coherent and had been searching for us for a while. The group we were sitting with was her family. A moment in time, Vanessa cherished a great deal. She explained she was sitting with her family earlier but got up to look for us. I asked Vanessa to sit for a while. I explained that being there together was a huge leap forward. I continued by explaining that our concentration level was still lacking, and it was imperative to keep each other in our thoughts. At which point, Vanessa spoke up and explained that as soon as she arrived in the park, she knew to concentrate on our faces but had no luck. Samuel reiterated he had been experiencing the same effect. Jasmine then spoke up and jokingly told us not to involve her. She was sleeping. She found her comments to be quite amusing, which made us all laugh. Sitting there and contemplating why they were just now having trouble calling on one another, I realized I was always present when contact was achieved, which got me to thinking maybe they were never able to conjure each other. The first time I encountered any of the group was when I met Vanessa in the jungle. Just before I ended up there. I was being pulled under the water by the sea creature with the tentacles. I, at that moment, thought about where Vanessa ended up. Then, when Vanessa and I were flying through the air into the bushes during our jungle experience, I caught myself thinking of Samuel and ended up on the plane. It was me. I was sure of it. I was the catalyst. I could conjure them up, but they could not do the same. I must have been able to call on the group due to them being under hypnosis. They were all linked up to me, and I was the only one in control. I enabled them to travel with me in this reality, leaping from dream to dream, where they could control their subconscious, but without me. Even if they somehow linked their dreams up with each other, they would not be conscious of it. I enabled them to wake from their dreams. While they were dreaming, they were no longer passengers. I felt confident that I alone could now control where we traveled, and anywhere we wanted to go, and I wanted to test my theory out immediately.

I asked the group to suggest a place they always wanted to visit. "Anywhere," they exclaimed.

Jasmine spoke up right away. She had always wanted to visit the Colosseum in Rome and pleaded with the group to agree. It apparently meant a lot to her, so without hesitation, we all agreed. I truly had no idea if it would work, but because of what we had experienced in the dream so far, I felt we were prepared for anything. I asked the group to hold each other's hands and close their eyes. Now imagine the Colosseum. I told them. Look around and focus. Listen to the noises. Try and imagine the different aromas in the air. We sat there in complete silence for just a moment with intense focus. I, being the curious one, decided to sneak a peek in hopes of seeing if anything different went. To my amazement, everything around me began melting away. The trees and people completely disintegrated before my eyes. Dogs running through the park were just gone. Everything quickly faded. For a second after, there was nothing around us at all, almost fog-like.

A moment later, erupting from the ground came thick ancient granite slabs, which quickly surrounded us. I watched as these monstrous blocks of history kept growing. Suddenly, without notice, handhold stairs, one by one, began to appear in endless rows of windows, forming themselves and completely engulfing us. Everybody's eyes were opened by that point. They all felt the earth rumble under their feet as the historic Colosseum grew, propelling us higher and higher. We all watched in amazement as this magnificent structure built itself up brick by brick. The exterior of the Colosseum was completely built, and the quaking eventually subsided. But just then, when we thought it was over, the stage area of the Colosseum down below began widening before our eyes and kept expanding. Huge ferocious lions appeared, roaring at the rustic barbaric gladiators. The authenticity of that ancient relic was absolutely astonishing. The monument was finally complete.

The seats just then began filling up with screaming Israelites dressed in dirty white togas thirsting for excitement. Roman soldiers were scattered throughout, guarding all the exits. I swear it was just like it looked in the movies. We sat there observing one person after another appear out of thin air, already cheering like they had been there for the entire time. I glanced over to see if Jasmine was enjoying herself when I realized she had on a white toga. We all did. The whole group was so excited and absolutely captivated. The smells were even authentic, which were a mix of body odor and testosterone with just a splash of death across the Colosseum. A king stood up and acknowledged the crowd. The crowd began to scream in anticipation, trying to appease the king so he would begin the festivities. King, being pleased with the response, let out a great bellow, "Let the games begin."

The crowd and I sat and watched the festivities for hours. Gladiators ripped the flesh off each other, chariots charging to their deaths, soldiers speared each other without hesitation, and all the while, crowds screamed for more. In my opinion, the whole ordeal was very barbaric. But Jasmine loved it. The games finally concluded. A good thing, too. I was beginning to feel a little nauseous. I thought I would have had a stronger stomach in a dream.

The group and I had been sleeping for some time. So while people are shouting at the Colosseum. I encouraged the group to gather around and take each other's hands so I could count us down. No sooner did I begin to count, visions of the chamber flashed in and out of focus, still holding each other's hands and the Colosseum. I had counted back to two and had a sensation of safely being back in the pod but still having flashes of the dream. The feeling was extremely intense. For a moment, I had second-guessed myself, wondering if I was actually in the pod or dreaming, but by the time I got to one, I was completely coherent and feeling elated. What I had just accomplished was beyond anything I could possibly hope for.

Will's voice sang through the speakers. You guys alright. That was intense. The chamber door opened, and Will sprinted over the chamber. Before I could exit, he grabbed my towel and, like a hyper puppy drooling all over me, asked what the hell we were doing because there was a point where my brain waves became extremely erratic. I reassured him that I was fine and then explained what I was able to create. Samuel, Jasmine, and Vanessa raced out of the pods, snagged a towel, and gathered around.

While I told the story, the whole group was entranced, like they were experiencing it all for the first time. Again, I think Will was in denial because it took the whole group to convince him that everything I said was actually happening. Will knew the machine was working, but manipulating it like I was astonished him, and he thought what he had just accomplished warranted celebration, even though it was six in the morning.

Behind the bar, I had a bottle of red wine from 1943 Cabernet. I kept it for a special occasion and thought the night we had just experienced would suffice. I got the bottle and uncorked it behind the bar. Holding the bottle with my four fingers, I managed to grab five glasses and one under my arm and carefully proceeded toward the table. I placed the glasses down, and the group gathered, excited as they were, they still managed to sit themselves down and watch me pour that rare bottle of aged wine—one glass at a time.

I decided a speech was in order, and I began by expressing how proud I was of them and how they exceeded all of my expectations. We raised our glasses and cheered to the future where night terrors no longer controlled our lives. When our glasses clinked together, immediately, I felt dizzy. I took a sip of my wine, trying to hide my ailment. After taking a swig, I gently placed my cup on the table and politely excused myself.

I headed to the washroom where I could be alone and turned on the water. While leaning over the sink, drenching my face with water, I began to have flashes of darkness like last time in the shower, where I experienced the same sensation. I quickly dropped to the floor, anticipating a blackout. Plus, I didn't want to create a scene crashing to the ground. I sat there for close to five minutes, just breathing, waiting for whatever was happening to pass. The feeling did eventually subside, and gingerly I picked myself up and peered into the mirror, making sure I didn't look ill or dying. Once I checked myself out and was sure I was fine, I rejoined the group.

I sat down at the table and took a sip of my wine, acting like nothing was wrong. The group was still excited and already talking about where they wanted to travel next. Vanessa was trying to convince Samuel that it was ladies first. No sooner did I sit down Vanessa, deciding to go over Samuel's head, asked me if she could choose the next adventure. Knowing Samuel was toying with her, I passed the buck and said they would have to decide for themselves. Samuel laughed, realizing she had no leverage. Then, being the gentleman, he caved immediately and agreed to let Vanessa choose.

The conversation was trivial compared to what I was really concerned with. I needed to know if any of the group was experiencing any of the same side effects. The blackouts I had experienced concerned me, and I was hoping they were unrelated to the experiment. I asked the group to grab their journals and, in detail, write everything they could remember. Even the smallest detail could be relevant, I told them. I then casually added that if they were to experience any side effects, such as dizzy spells, or loss of consciousness, I would need to be informed immediately. I then asked if anyone had exuded anything similar to those symptoms to date, but everyone seemed fine. They swore they felt wonderful and refreshed. Will, worried about my questioning, asked if I experienced anything similar to what I described. I'm not sure why I lied to him, but I said I was good to go. I guess nothing was going to stop this experiment. Not even me.

Chapter Fourteen

Months had gone by experimenting. We went three times a week, never missing a session. With my creative ability, I had complete control over our reality and developed a bit of a God complex. I had the power to build anything just by imagining, from the Pyramids in Egypt to the Eiffel Towers in Paris.

I created them. The group's concentration had been perfected. They weren't able to call on each other, but they were able to differentiate reality from their dream state immediately after going under. Plus, their night terrors no longer haunt them, making the experiment a complete success. Will and I were already talking about taking on more patients.

Now that I understood how to reach the subjects in the dream state, I assumed I would be able to help them that much faster. The group anticipated the experiment was coming to an end. I explained to them that there were a lot of people with night terrors that needed my help. The group knew immediately I was giving the 'it's not you, it's me' speech, which for the group, felt bittersweet. I imagine nobody wanted the sessions to end, but at least they were cured and sleeping through the night.

My blackouts were still occurring, and I felt like they were more frequent. I'd gone to see my doctor concerned, but after a few tests and an MRI, he reassured me I was fine and cleared me with a clean health bill. I was quite relieved, to say the least. I was expecting him to return and tell me I had a tumor or something. I had to just chalk it up to myself being overly exhausted after using certain parts of my subconscious and connecting with the subjects during REM sleep. I could now see how I would become mentally drained. A few weeks had passed, and I decided to begin interviewing patients for the next experiment. I had already met with several candidates, but none of them fit the criteria I was looking for until I met Susan Shepherd. I chose her because she had a fear of water. I guess choosing her was more therapeutic for me than for her.

I also had a fear of water since I was a child, and when Susan Shepherd explained her night terror, she conjured up past fears in me that had been dormant for some time. Before I told her I was taking her on, I enlightened her to the fact that we both had the same fear, and if she wanted, we would tackle it together.

Susan was in her 30s. She had been married for a couple of years and just had her first baby, which they named Julius. He was an adorable little guy with big blue eyes and bright red hair. I thought he was the coolest kid ever. He had me at 'gaga'.

The next patient I decided to treat was Jamal Washington. His night terrors involved being buried alive when he went into detail regarding his dreams. He mentioned he would stop breathing in his sleep and often awoke choking, fighting to catch his breath on many occasions.

Jamal and his wife worried about his safety and were hoping I could help. I was more than pleased to take him on as a patient. I found his condition to be life-threatening and was exactly the type of case I had anticipated since I began my practice. I needed to recruit one more subject for the next group to be complete. It took about a week, but I finally found him.

His name was Richard Dresler. His situation was the most severe case I had yet to come across. His night terrors concerned his children, and him losing sight of them for just a moment when he realized the building he was in was being demolished within mere minutes. He continued explaining that during his frantic search, he would hear the ticking of a timer counting down. And the closer he got to rescuing his children, the louder the ticking became.

The truly disturbing part that concerned me was he was a sleepwalker and had gone as far as to leave his house. Richard stated that on a few occasions, he awoke, finding himself curled up in a park under a play structure. This happened to him several times, ending up in unfamiliar places, and with him being a single father, he needed to find a way to curb his disorder. His children were only five and eight years old. His wife died in a horrific car accident a couple of years back, and he felt like he was just going through the motions ever since.

Not to lessen the severity of the situation, but it reminded me of that movie with Tom Hanks, *Sleepless in Seattle*. The second group was finally set in place. One by one, I introduced them to the chambers and explained their function and how those shiny silver cylindrical masterpieces were going to be able to perform their magic. Following my morality speech, almost everything was perfect. The only obstacle that Will and I were faced with was concerning Jamal.

The night terrors that he had been experiencing manifested themselves into an acute case of claustrophobia. Knowing he would have to submerge himself and trust us completely conjured up reservations with the entire process, problems like this were anticipated, and since I had no patience for his meandering, I decided to call out the big guns and introduced Jamal to Will. Will had a calm demeanor and had a knack for easing the patience. Will definitely have a special talent, one that I obviously never inherited. Dealing with the emotions of my subjects was equivalent to chewing glass.

Will took Jamal aside while Jasmine and I sat at the bar. She and I cared for each other so much, but we were becoming distant from all the work I had to do, which left me little to no time for her. She often expressed her feelings of becoming idle and wasting her time watching me waste mine unless things were to change. I knew the inevitability. Jasmine had recently inherited a substantial amount of money from her grandfather's passing, and I think she began to feel trapped with me. There was nothing I could do to make the situation better either. I couldn't and wouldn't quit my job, so I knew it was only a matter of time before she ended it. She couldn't even look me in the eye anymore. But I still loved her; the last thing I wanted to do was hold her back.

Jasmine and I decided to play a pool game while Will performed the magic.

Convincing Jamal to proceed with the experiment seemed to take longer than anticipated. Jasmine and I were on the third game when he observed Will handing Jamal a bathing suit. Will then fix up the machine while Jamal went to change. Will had been such an asset to the experiment. The first time I entered the pods, it was Will's voice that got me through.

Now watching him with Jamal made me realize he was as imperative to this experiment as I was. Jamal reluctantly exited the change room. He still seemed apprehensive about the situation because he had trouble looking at either of us, so I personally escorted him to the open chamber. I reassured him once again that I had performed this experiment many times and there was nothing to be nervous about. I also reminded him why he was there in the first place to curb his fears for good.

Jamal nodded, agreeing with me, and nervously entered the chamber. Will let Jamal get comfortable with the pod before he proceeded any further. I stood at the pod's opening the entire time, ensuring he was completely relaxed. Jamal was the one to actually ask Will to close the pod door, which reassured us he felt safe and was ready to face his fear. The chamber door began to close, encasing him.

Will communicated with Jamal through the entire process, which didn't take long, for we were just taking the first step that day which was getting Jamal in that pod. He stayed in there for close to ten minutes, which was surprising. He just laid there, still listening to Will tell jokes. I think at one point, Jamal got lost in the moment and forgot where he was because Jasmine and I heard him just howling in laughter. After experiencing the chamber, Jamal was more than confident he could proceed, and with him being the last piece of the puzzle, we were set.

I had one final session with my initial group, which was that very night, and their time with me will be complete. There was nothing else to teach them. I was going to reinforce everything that they had learned that night. I decided to do something special to see them off instead. After Jamal and Will left, Jasmine and I got into a very heated discussion.

She realized I had been distant with her and wanted to know what was happening. I was not one to play games, so I laid it all out. I explained I had no time for anything with new patients coming in would become unbearable. I expressed my love for her but suggested she search for someone that would make her feel as special as the woman I knew she was. When I first met Jasmine, she was tired and a mess, but with all the work we had accomplished with her night terrors, it was like she had a new lease on life.

I didn't need to convince her it was the right move. She knew it was. We headed into the bathroom as tears bottled up in Jasmine's eyes. She began apologizing for it not working and knew she had been distant also. After all the help I had given her, she felt selfish for even thinking of leaving and wasn't sure what she should do.

I was completely shattered by what I had to do, but I knew it was the best for us. I apparently was the best break-up artist ever because ending the relationship was pretty easy.

Jasmine and I lay on my bed for hours, holding each other. I think neither of us wanted to let go because of what was coming next. When we finally did let go, I wiped a lingering tear from her eye and kissed her passionately for the last time. I then told her I had to go downstairs to set up, but I just needed to distance myself before becoming emotional.

Just before I left the room, Jasmine told me she was leaving to try and reunite with her father. She continued saying she would not be participating in our last session and was grateful for everything I had done for her. With a lump in my throat, realizing our last day together was just cut short, I agreed that seeing her father was a good idea and wished her the very best. I abruptly turned around and darted for the basement. I sat downstairs for a couple of hours, drowning my sorrows in gin and tonic, listening to Jasmine walking around upstairs, packing up her things, and finally leaving when I heard the door closed behind her. I ran upstairs to watch her get into her car and exit my life forever.

When I could no longer see her car, I sobbed all the way to my room, crashed down on my bed, and fell asleep until Will arrived. It was close to six in the evening. When Will got there I was still asleep. He told me he chimed the doorbell for close to five minutes before he decided to use the spare key in the mailbox. He knew where the key was because I was running late with my patients a couple of months back, and Will was due to come by to perform maintenance. I thought I had trusted him with my life, so I didn't see why I couldn't trust him with my home.

I woke up with Will hovering over my bed, tapping me on the shoulder. For just a moment, I thought it was Jasmine, but when the fact that her and I had just broken up flooded my thoughts, my eyes sprung open, and I sat up to see it was

Will. He began apologizing for letting himself in, but he saw my car in the driveway hoping everything was okay.

I told him I appreciated his friendship again, telling him that Jasmine was no longer in the group. He knew her leaving the group was not the whole story. He told me to get dressed and meet him in the basement. Will was sitting at the table when I got down there. He had a bottle of Jack Daniels with him and two shot glasses. Plus, there were two big gaggers pre-roll placed together on the table waiting for me. He told me later that night he knew Jasmine and I had ended our relationship because of the redness around my eyes when he woke me. As much as I wanted to hide my feelings, it was nearly impossible to hide a broken heart. Will and I sat there and drank the whole bottle of Jack shot by shot. Plus, I already smoked a joint. He rolled, and his task was complete. It was so inevitable. I was like, Jasmine, who? There was no way I was going forward with the experiment that night.

Will convinced me to call the gang and invite them over for farewell drinks. It wasn't imperative anymore to go under because the group was cured of their terrors. That night was more for entertainment, but I knew they would empathize because of my mental state. Samuel and Vanessa came by and had no problem with just socializing. Vanessa told me that night Jasmine had phoned her and filled her in on the details.

Jasmine just phoned to say goodbye, but you know how women talk. Vanessa asked if I would be okay and said Jasmine wanted to know but not to let off that she was asking for her. Vanessa told me because she didn't like to lie. I was fine, I told her and said that things happen, then abruptly asked if she changed the subject due to the night being a joyous occasion. She knew I was hurting but respected my wishes and asked me to dance.

Samuel and Will just sat there wooing us and coaxing us to dance dirty. We were doing fine ignoring them until Vanessa grabbed my behind and asked the boys if that was what they wanted. It just made them holler louder. The whole show they put on was for my benefit.

They knew I needed to get my mind thinking of something other than Jasmine; they were successful, too. I had a great time that night. After Vanessa and my dance was over, Samuel decided to cut and gave me a chance to sit with Will and talk. He also probed to see if I would be fine, but Will knew he had a legitimate claim. He and I worked together, and if I were to screw up in any capacity, he would be the one to have to clean up the mess.

Chapter Fifteen

I woke up the next morning in the basement, draped across the pool table. Will and Vanessa were still awake, sitting at the bar, talking. I wasn't sure, but it looked like they were getting chummy with each other because their demeanor quickly changed when I sat up from the pool table. I also saw Will blush. I think Vanessa also felt a little awkward because she quickly located her purse and said she had to go.

Vanessa called out to Samuel due to him being her ride. I remember looking around, but he was nowhere to be found, and then I glanced over to the chambers and realized one was open. I walked over and peeked in, and there, snoring away while bobbing up and down, was Samuel. I'm unsure if it was as funny as I made it out to be. Maybe I just needed to release some anxiety, but I almost peed in my pants.

My laughing episode woke Samuel, and when it finally became clear to him that laughter was directed at him, he frantically leaped out of the chamber, freezing cold. He swiftly changed into his clothes, thanked me for another eventful night, and left to drive Vanessa home. Not wanting to discuss what I witnessed with him and Vanessa, Will decided to leave right behind. No sooner did the door close behind them than thoughts of Jasmine leaving began to saturate me. I knew dwelling on the situation would almost paralyze me, and I would just end up sleeping, so I decided to go see the only two people I felt comfortable talking with, my parents.

I arrived just around lunchtime, knowing my mom would insist on making me a hearty meal. There was nothing she loved more than for her little scientist, as she liked to refer to me to come home to visit. She always began with wanting to feed me and probe me with questions to ensure I was taking care of myself. I had to admit I enjoyed the attention. I would never tell her that, but I did.

It always astonished me that no matter how old or educated I had become, I would always feel like that little boy when Mummy cuddled me. Life is difficult so to have a place like home where all your worries could disappear, even if it was just for a few hours, was invaluable to me. I could always put things in perspective with the help of my parents. It took an hour to arrive. When I pulled into the driveway, my dad was washing his Ford truck.

There was nothing he loved more than his cerulean blue four x four. If we let him, he would talk about that hunk of metal all night long. Before I moved out on my own, I constantly teased him that he was cheating on Mom with that truck. The best part was my dad's retort – he used to always reply with the same joke because it made my mom giggle and me blush.

He said if Mom had the traction that the Ford had, he would ride her just as much. I stepped out of my car and greeted my dad. With a big smile, he threw down a sponge and walked up to me, and shook my hand. He asked how work was going and wondered if everything was okay. I felt so messed up that I was compelled to let it fly.

We stood out for nearly twenty minutes, discussing Jasmine and me ending it, contemplating whether I made the right move. My dad just listened, letting me vent, knowing that I was just trying to make sense of my choices. After we talked, he encouraged me to go say hi to my mom. She had just made braciole and was keeping it warm, waiting for my dad to finish with his truck. I walked in and called out for my mom, acknowledging my presence.

She let out a howling scream and rushed toward me, planting an enormous hug on me, followed by one of her kisses that left her lipstick smeared all over my cheek, which always stayed there until the moment I left. She would take that opportunity to wipe it off herself and have one last chance to ensure I took care of myself immediately. She asked if I were hungry and told me to sit. She didn't have to tell me twice. She had some of the best recipes I have ever tasted.

Dowling out the braciole, she asked what was wrong. I was never able to mask misery or pain around my mother. She had a sixth sense or something. When I told her about Jasmine and me breaking up, she hugged me and again agreed that my work was more important and that I had made the right decision. She continued saying that for me to let anything get in the way of the experiments when being so close to my objective would be irresponsible.

She was absolutely right, too, because if my machine worked as successfully as it did with the first group on every other group after, I could seriously change the way the world slept.

Before I left my parents, I decided to use the washroom, knowing it was a long ride home. But while I was in there, I experienced yet another blackout. I was sitting down already, so that particular episode wasn't as difficult to control but felt different from the other times. I knew I was sitting in the washroom, but I felt like I was being forced into a dream state.

A few minutes went by with me cradling my head in my hands and focusing on a floor stain, but I managed to pull myself together. Driving home, I couldn't shake what had just happened. My hypothesis was that during my temporary blackout, I must have instinctively tried to control my subconscious on some level due to the sensation of almost going under, which made it feel like a dream state.

I got back home around five. Will was arriving at six, and I wanted him to help me decide what to order for dinner.

It was important to make a good impression on the group and put them at ease quickly. In my experience, a hearty meal always did the trick. Will arrived a little after seven.

That was the first time he had ever been late, making me curious why. When I asked him what held him up, he said he was on a date and lost track of time.

At first, I thought he was lying to me because Will never said anything about meeting anyone, and we talked about everything. I asked if the date went well and if it were serious. He responded, saying it was their first date and they were taking it slow. At that moment, everything fell into place. He was deliberately dodging telling me her name and was vague on the details.

He had a date with Vanessa, and I saw that spark between those two this morning. I neglected to say anything. He would have told me if he wanted me to know, so I changed the subject and asked what we would order for dinner. After throwing some ideas out there, will and I decided on Chinese food. I thought it was a perfect choice.

I don't think a billion people could be wrong. Will decided to warm up the machines so he and I could play pool, enjoy a couple of drinks, waiting for the new group to arrive. While playing pool, I had a weak moment and couldn't resist. I knew it was Vanessa he was seeing so nonchalantly. I asked when he was going to see her next.

Stunned at what I had just said, Will looked up and stared at me for a few seconds before he uttered in a shaky voice. He whispered who as he tried to play with a tooth. I stared right back at him and repeated her name. Vanessa, I reiterated. Will began to blush, knowing the jig was up, then asked how I knew.

I explained it was his body language, plus the fact that he turned a ripe tomato red every time her name was mentioned. I didn't make a big deal out of it. I just hope he was happy and told him I was glad he found someone. He explained that he would have told me, but because of what happened with Jasmine, he didn't find it appropriate. I appreciated his concern but told him I was okay, and I felt genuinely happy for him. I honestly believed he needed and deserved it.

The first member of the group to arrive was Richard. His babysitter released him early, and he had nothing better to do, so he came by. I was intrigued he was there early. It gave Will and me a chance to get to know him on a personal level.

I offered him a drink and challenged him to a game of pool as soon as I cleaned the floor with Will. Will didn't even trash talk anymore. It was funny. He, at that point, knew I owned that table.

I had shown him many tricks and pointers, which he never seemed to grasp. But what he did learn was trash talking. He just had to sharpen up his game. Will and I were almost through. He knew I was a good player but always acted like he had a chance to beat me today, with no exception, but I don't think he was about to let on to Richard how good I was. I think he wanted me to just sink all the balls on Richard. Really embarrass him because through the entire game Will kept complaining. I could have made shots I intentionally missed to give Richard a chance. I guess Will forgot how I used to play him when we first met.

We sat around playing pool and drinking until the rest of the group arrived. Richard seemed to genuinely be a sincere gentleman who loved his children greatly. His sole purpose was to get well so his children would never become exposed to his sleepwalking. Everything we talked about reverted to his children. It is unprofessional to get emotionally involved in patients' personal lives, but Richard was very likable, and I felt compelled to begin with him first.

I wouldn't let on to the other subjects, but Richard became my pet project. It was close to nine when my doorbell chimed. I was sitting sipping my drink while Richard and Will were playing the longest game of pool I think I had ever witnessed. So I opted to run and get to the door. It was Susan.

She was early and looked ready to go. I felt a little nervousness on her part, but all in all, she was excited to begin. I escorted her to the basement and told her I would be down momentarily. I took that opportunity to order. The Chinese food where I ordered from.

It only took twenty minutes to deliver, and we were still waiting for Jamal. I assumed he wasn't far behind. I finished ordering and scooted downstairs but made it halfway when the doorbell chimed again; it was Jamal. When I opened the door, he seemed less enthusiastic to be there. I felt a lot of hesitation from him but said nothing.

I just got him to the basement and decided my strategy for him was to get him liquored up. I explained to the group that it was my practice to get to know one another before starting the experiment. The group appeared pleased. There would be some downtime before we jumped right in, and at that point, we heard a quiet sigh of relief from Jamal. I wasn't worried.

I was sure he'd be fine. Jamal liked his rum. I told Will secretly to keep topping him up so he wouldn't pose a problem during the experiment. Will chuckled and asked if that was ethical. I chuckled right back and asked when we started doing things ethically.

The doorbell chimed once again. Chinese food had arrived. Will opted to answer the door this time. He had met Woo Long a few times and now had a dialogue going with him, just like always. Will, being oblivious, stayed at the door, chatting for close to ten minutes, not realizing our food was getting cold.

Will had made his way to the basement, and the group seemed thrilled. Woo and his family never disappointed either. The food was mouthwatering; the sake was nice and spicy. Plus, by the time we finished, Jamal didn't have a nervous bone in his body. I grabbed the rum off the table, topped it up in everyone's glass, and toasted to the experiment's success.

Everyone began cheering and clinking their glasses. I then looked to Will, motioning with my eyes that it was a perfect time to begin.

Like always, he nodded, got up, and performed his magic. Will started over to the chambers and opened the lids. I asked everyone to proceed to the towel rack where their bathing suits were set out for them.

Susan sprinted over, eager to begin. Richard and Jamal got up slowly but eventually caught up to her. I followed right behind, already undressing. By the time I got to the towel rack, I was completely nude. Susan let out a gasp and looked away, which prompted me to explain to them this was a regular occurrence.

Instead of using the change room one at a time, we would just change there to conserve time. We were all adults. I exclaimed no leering would be permitted. A sudden shock wore off, and they all changed into their suits. The pod doors were opened and waiting on us to enter the chambers.

I reiterated that at any minute, for any reason, they wanted out to just speak into the microphone, and Will would open those doors. I reassured them once again that there was nothing to fear and that we would be together every step of the way. Everyone was enclosed in their chamber. Jamal and Susan chose the two closest to Will, and

Richard and I settled for the other two. I remember feeling so in control, lying there this time around, knowing I had the knowledge and experience.

It exhilarated me. Real soft, smoky voice poured through the speakers. "Okay, gang, here we go." And the doors began to close, just like always. Darkness engulfed the chamber, and everything went silent.

Will then decided to ask Jamal in a loud, bellowing voice how he was feeling, which scared the piss out of me. Jamal responded by screaming not to yell because Will's voice also startled him. Will then encouraged us to brace ourselves for the electricity. I was used to the sudden jolt by then and was now anticipating the screams from the others. Will also enjoyed that part.

I giggled every time I heard them yell and yell they did. Will flicked the switch, and the howls came pouring through the speakers. I could faintly hear Will bellowing. While we simultaneously cringed.

The group and I lay there for a few minutes, adapting to the constant flow of electricity coursing through our bodies. I felt they were prepped and asked if everyone was coherent. When they acknowledged they were fine, I prompted them to get ready for the best ride of their life. It was a go on all fronts, and eagerly I proceeded with the hypnosis. Like the previous group, I began the same way as water splashed against their bodies bobbing up and down.

Imagine, I encouraged them to picture their bodies bobbing up and down in the chambers as the water splashed against their bodies bobbing up and down. Imagine yourself floating, drifting; I told them with not a worry in the world as we go up and down. At that point, I asked them to envision being aboard a sailboat, riding the heavy sea waves still bobbing up and down. The moment I knew that they were mine, I introduced the bright lights shining in the distance and encouraged them to head toward it, repeating repeatedly until they were completely under. Will recognize from their brainwaves that the group was under and began with the sleep inducer.

Will's voice whispered through the speaker one last time before he injected us. I'll see you soon, sir, he uttered as I felt the needle penetrate my neck, not more than a momentary lapse. And I, too was out.

Chapter Sixteen

The first thing I can recall after opening my eyes was this brilliant, blinding light. I couldn't make out anything, but I was still coherent about the fact that I was dreaming.

The first thing I decided to attempt was conjuring up the team. I thought of them and called their names one by one as they appeared before me like magic. The light was ferociously bright, and the crew was battling to keep their eyes open. So I decided at that point to create a little café I had once visited in Barcelona with my ex-girlfriend. But while attempting it, I realized the building appeared in the far distance instead of around us. I recognized the effort it took for me to create anything for quite some time was getting difficult, but this was the first time we had to travel to see one of my creations. The group didn't realize there was a problem, but they still weren't thrilled to walk through this blinding white light. They complained all the way to the coffee shop. All I recall when reaching the shop was a feeling of relief because at least now they would stop all their complaining.

At last, we sat, and I took the opportunity to explain the dream world could be manipulated. I continued explaining that it was their sole purpose to learn how to manipulate their dreams and control them that was why they were there, to know the difference between dreams and reality. Once they obtained that ability, I exclaimed, their night terrors would cease to exist.

Jamal was completely beside himself. He wasn't convinced he was dreaming of hiking toward the café. I actually had to remind him three times that we were all in the chambers. I couldn't understand why it was so difficult to grasp. We were all walking on what looked like clouds, for goodness sake, not to mention going for coffee at the only standing building anywhere.

I began to observe that the longer the subjects were under, the more difficult it became for them to remain focused. I could tell it was their first trip.

Richard, at that moment, began to panic, screaming for his children. He actually asked us to help in locating them. I asked Richard to sit back down. Susan and Jamal, now agitated, were worried for Richard and demanded we search for his children. I snickered and asked for them to take a seat. Panicked and frustrated, they reluctantly agreed. I began explaining that to cure the night terrors, they had to see them for what they really were. I reminded Richard his babysitter was taking care of his children and that everything was fine. When I asked him to recall the chambers we were floating in, he was able to calm himself, to win him over completely. I asked the group to watch as I created out of thin air an old reminiscent ice cream parlor right across from where we were sitting, another monument from my past that had great significance for me, hoping my energy would sustain. I began brick by brick. The parlor grew, molding into whatever I envisioned. It was a place I used to frequent with my dad when I was just a kid. The building was painted in all sorts of colors of the rainbow. It was a place where I still felt like a child. When the structure was complete, Susan looked at me, pleading with her eyes for me to let her get an ice cream cone. I exclaimed that it was her dream and she could do whatever she desired.

Richard, Jamal, and I sat at the cafe talking about how I was able to conjure up the structure. I really had no answer. All I knew was I was able to.

In my opinion, these were questions I didn't need to know the answers to. My experiment was working, and I was fine with that. The amount of energy I was using to hold all of us together while we were dreaming was why I thought my blackouts were happening. Conjuring up monuments and traveling to God knows where would drain my energy at a more accelerated rate.

I decided with this group; my ego would not interfere. I refused to show off anymore. I knew the blackouts would subside if I took it easy. Hence the café and the ice cream parlor. Not the wow factor the group was expecting, but effective all the same. After the experiment concluded for the night, I sent everyone home and told them I would see them next week.

Ten minutes later, just like clockwork, I felt lightheaded but fought through it. In my opinion, not passing out was a win. I felt like I was getting it under control, and it was only a matter of time before I became blackout-free. It was like any other muscle. The more you work it, the stronger it will become.

For the next few sessions, I decided to take my own advice and perform small acts for the group. At that point, I felt like a real bad magician performing tricks that would make a roomful of children fall asleep. My methods were working, which was my primary concern.

The new group had told me their dreams were not as intense as they were before they came to see me. Jamal was sleeping through the night without choking. Richard said he hadn't had a sleepwalking episode since, and Susan actually went swimming the other day with her son. I was more than pleased with the results. I just felt like there was more I could accomplish. But I was being held back by the fear of my blackouts. I was reduced to creating movie theaters, cafes, and ice cream parlors.

I recall the last place we went before I heard the terrible news. Due to Susan's reoccurring night terror involving water, the group and I spent a lot of time in the deep end of the pool Susan used to frequent as a child. It was also the place where she acquired her fear of water. A couple of bullies were roughhousing and kept dunking her underwater.

They went too far, and she lost consciousness. The lifeguard revived her, but since that day, the water became the monster in her closet. Susan was a godsend. I don't think I would have even faced that fear if it wasn't for her. I thought Susan and everyone else that came to me, facing their fears, were extremely brave, more courageous than I could have ever been.

The end of that particular session was like no other. I counted everyone down, just like always. But by the time I got to one, I still felt like I was in a dream. This sensation lasted for a few minutes. Will actually came over and poked his head in the chamber to see if I was okay. I told him I was fine and just thinking of the next session, but he knew I wasn't being truthful.

We all changed our clothes and wrote in our journals. From the group's energy, they seem to have had a great night. They even looked healthier than they did when we first met.

I remember feeling a sense of pride that morning. The only thing I had ever wanted to do in the world that I felt passionate about was now coming true. I could genuinely help.

After we finished our journals, I saw everyone out and sprawled out on the couch. I was wide awake and had nothing to do, so I did what anyone would have done with all that free time. I grabbed the remote again, watching TV for an hour. I sat there surfing, searching for anything that would draw my attention. That was when a news broadcast came on that caught my eye.

A young woman was supposedly thrown from the 40th floor of the Empire State building downtown. Immediately, my heart fell into my stomach. I couldn't fathom how anyone could do something so horrifying. Like my first thought was that whoever was capable of such an atrocity should be executed because the terror that individual must have felt before they plunged to their death must have been horrendous. I was fixated with the story as it continuously ran through my mind. The news anchor just then said they received information on the identity of the victim and the perpetrator. When they viewed the victim's picture, I swear I almost threw up. The news anchor said it was a family dispute between father and daughter, and the father apparently threw his daughter out the window. The name of the victim was Jasmine Clyde. When I heard the name, I was sure I heard wrong. But when the picture appeared on the screen, I instantly fell to my knees and sobbed uncontrollably, feeling empty and completely helpless.

I recall at that moment thinking it possibly could have been a misunderstanding. I got to my feet, ran to the phone, and called Vanessa. I knew Jasmine and she were friends, so if anything happened, she would have had to have heard it.

When Vanessa answered, she was crying. I told her it was me, and she began to cry harder. At that point, reality sunk in, and I began to cry with her. I knew it. Jasmine was gone, still crying. I demanded Vanessa tell me what had happened. All she knew was that Jasmine was meeting her dad at work because he wanted to take her to lunch. That was the last time she talked with Jasmine. Then she saw the news. I then asked where Jasmine's dad was because I needed answers. I needed to know how he could have done this to the only woman I ever loved.

I knew Jasmine and her dad had been estranged for a while, but nothing she told me about her father led me to believe he hated her enough to perform such an atrocity.

Vanessa told me he was being detained and was trying to come up with the bail. She also said she had been in contact with Jasmine's mother and would let us know when the funeral was. I told Vanessa to keep me informed and to relay any new information to Will, so I would always be up to date. I let Vanessa go immediately and phoned the number of the prison where they were holding Mr. Clyde. When I phoned, I was denied access but was able to put my name on a list that entitled me to see him in a couple of days.

I paced through my house for hours, invoking every emotion and running through every scenario of how Mr. Clyde could have done this to his own daughter; when, without warning, I became dizzy. Everything went dark.

The next thing I know, I woke up to the doorbell chiming. It was Will coming to check on me. When I let him in, he asked where I was because he had been chiming for ten minutes. I asked why he didn't use the spare key. He said he took it home and forgot it there. I apologized and, laying there, said I was sleeping. I suddenly peered at the clock on the wall and realized I had been out for a few hours. That was the worst blackout I had to date. The stress I felt about Jasmine put me over the edge, and I knew I had to calm myself down. After that blackout and what happened to Jasmine, I wasn't even worried about the experiment. I had been working with the second group long enough for them to have complete control and dream. After what had happened, I was sure they would understand. I explained to Will that for now, we would stop but possibly reconvene at a later date. He knew I was destroyed by what happened to Jasmine and agreed it was for the best.

He went on to ask how I was doing otherwise. He said he saw a change in my behavior some time ago and wondered what else was happening. Nobody knew I was having blackouts, so he became upset with me when I told him. He exclaimed that helping people was a noble profession, but not at the cost of my life. When I told him the blackouts began after the very first test run, he was beside himself. I think at one point, he wanted to slug me, but instead, he just said he was extremely disappointed that I didn't trust him enough to let him in on my ailment. I felt so stupid for what I did. I don't know why I didn't tell him. I guess I felt it could have postponed the experiment, and the thirst for my success blinded me. Will eventually calmed himself, and we began talking about Jasmine. He came by because Vanessa had found out the date for the funeral. It was July 26 to 3 p.m. When he told me the date, I felt reality sucker punch me right in the gut, making my eyes puddle with tears. Will, realizing the pain I must have been experiencing, grabbed me and just hugged me. We stood there for a few minutes, just hugging and expressing how very sorry he was.

Will was my best friend, and I was his. The pain I felt affected him deeply, which is why he stayed with me the entire night talking. We just drank and played pool. Also, I think he was worried that I would do something foolish; in retrospect, he wasn't far off.

During one of our games, the phone rang, I ran up to answer, and to my surprise, it was Samuel. I hadn't heard from him for a while, and for a second, I was thrilled until he asked if I had been watching the news without warning. I began crying again. Samuel immediately joined in and began to cry, trying to apologize for bringing it up. I told him there was no need to apologize. I know it was a trying time for everyone involved. I continued saying how wonderful it was to hear from him and wanted him to come over and hang out with the boys as much as he wanted to; he had to fly out the following day for work, so he needed his sleep. He already knew when the funeral was and guaranteed me he would see us there. He said his goodbyes and let me go.

I went back downstairs and finished the games that I was playing with Will.

After I won the game, I grabbed a bottle of scotch from the bar. Will and I drank until we passed out.

A few days went by with me, racking my brain to how Jasmine's father could have done this to her. I was finally going to confront him that day and remember feeling nervous when I walked into the prison.

I signed my name and was escorted through the building. We passed through six doors, all with the highest security. The room they brought me to had ten cubicles side by side. The guard directed me to cubicle eight. I slowly crept across the room, eyeing all the other inmates sitting with their visitors. Everyone was rough, looking like they were exactly where they were supposed to be. When I reached cubicle eight, all I saw was this old man with heartbreak on his face. When he looked up at me, he knew who I was. Jasmine had shown him pictures of me and apparently talked about me quite often. All I could do at first was stare at him. Everything I wanted to ask him eluded me.

At that point, I felt like an imbecile standing there, leering at him. Mr. Clyde, knowing I was feeling awkward, motioned for me to pick up the phone. Gingerly, I sat down and put the phone to my ear, in a soft, pathetic voice. Mr.

Clyde introduced himself and asked how I was feeling. I responded, saying, not well for the simple fact that he just killed my ex-girlfriend. No sooner did I say that did Mr. Clyde completely fall apart. He said he had no recollection of the event with his daughter. He remembers her surprising him by covering his eyes while he was working. She rushed him to finish up so they could go to lunch. The last thing he remembered, he said, was grabbing his jacket. He said the next thing he knew; he was standing in front of a broken window looking out. It startled him enough that he fell backward on his behind and began to back away from the window. He immediately looked around for Jasmine when he realized everyone was screaming and scrambling to get out of the office, which he said to the police after they arrested him. That was all he remembered.

I was very good at reading people, and nothing about Mr. Clyde said he could have done this, but the reality is he did do this. Could it have been some sort of seizure? And the seizure resulted in the death of his daughter. As much as I wanted him to pay for what he had done, I just couldn't. Jasmine was too important to me to let her dad deal with this alone.

The first thing I decided to do was use my pull in the psychiatric community to have a complete evaluation of Mr. Clyde and see if it was possible that a seizure could have caused his episode.

Chapter Seventeen

It was 9:30 in the morning when I awoke. The smell of nabob filled the room, which lured me out of bed. I felt reluctant because that was the day of the funeral. With little desire, I sprung to my feet and took a shower.

As the water beaded off my head, I recalled a moment when Jasmine and I were taking a shower. I was standing behind her, washing her hair, telling her jokes that I made up myself. The one joke I remember making her laugh the most was the one about John Lennon; God rest his soul. It went like this, "What was the last thing John Lennon said before he was shot? Answer, 'Oh, no'." I remember her turning around and slapping me, telling me I was bad. And then she just laughed. She had the most intoxicating laugh.

I finished up in the bathroom and went downstairs, poured myself a cup of coffee. I sat down there till close to one in the afternoon, just thinking and waiting to catch up to reality. I knew I was waiting for the funeral to confirm what I already knew.

There was a point when I was sitting there in the basement, thinking if I didn't go, maybe she would never be dead to me. I could pretend she just left and we never saw each other again. Or maybe she moved overseas and started a new life. The best one was she began skating again and made it to the Olympics. I was grinning ear to ear, just thinking, what if.

I was prompted to run upstairs due to the phone ringing. It was Vanessa calling, telling me a limousine was coming to pick me up at around two, so Will, Vanessa, and I could all go together. I told her I was ready and would be waiting for their arrival. Before I let her go, I mentioned that Samuel was aware of what happened and was attending. Vanessa said she had been trying to contact him but couldn't get a hold of him. He must have been out with his family.

One thing I know about Samuel, he was never late.

I just told Vanessa to keep with the schedule, and if we couldn't contact him, I was sure he would meet us at the funeral. I tried Samuel a few more times but got nothing.

Two o'clock rolled around when the limo pulled up. I threw on my jacket and reluctantly walked out to greet them. I got to the sidewalk, and the car door opened. Vanessa was compelled to jump out and hug me tight. She kissed me on the cheek and expressed how very sorry she felt for everything again, and we both began to cry. Vanessa pulled away, and looked me in the eye while wiping away a tear falling from my cheek with her hand on my back. She motioned for us to get going.

I got into the limousine first and Vanessa right behind, still with her hand on my back. Will was already in the car and greeted me with a simple handshake. The entire ride, we were completely silent. I just peered out the window, staring at the trees.

It was windy that day, so the trees were dancing in sequence. Everything seemed to be moving at such a slow pace. The ride seemed like it lasted forever. But eventually, we arrived.

The cemetery was full of other limousines and black sedans. Everyone was wearing black suits and garments, shaking hands and hugging each other. A dark feeling engulfed us all that day, bringing us closer together. I hardly knew a soul there, but everyone seemed to know me. The love and sympathy I received from everyone were overwhelming. When I met Jasmine's mother, she ran to me, and we embraced for over five minutes, just crying. When she caught her breath, she said that Jasmine was completely in love with me and wished things could have been different. Mrs. Clyde said I was the best thing that ever happened to her, and she was glad that Jasmine had a chance to be happy. I really had no idea what to say. She had rendered me speechless. I had no idea Jasmine felt so strongly for me. I felt so stupid for breaking the relationship off with her. Me being a psychologist, I should have known how she felt. I knew it was the experiment that made me end it. I guess at the time; I cared more about my own success than I did her. I didn't anymore. I remember thinking I would destroy that damn machine just to see her one last time.

The funeral began, and the priest was reciting a passage out of the Bible. I don't recall which one, but it was elegant.

Jasmine looked beautiful. So still laying there. I had such a compulsion to just pull her out of there and demand that she wake up. But reality had finally set in, and I knew I would never see her again after today. As I closed my eyes, I recall saying one last goodbye to her. "Goodbye," I said.

The funeral was just finishing. Some people began walking back to their cars, while others stayed behind to say their final words. The coffin was slowly lowered to the ground. I reached down and grabbed a handful of dirt. As I threw the dirt on Jasmine's casket, I wished her well on her journey and hoped I would one day see her again.

I quickly regained my composure and proceeded to the limousine. The ride home was more exciting than I had anticipated. Will had stocked up the mini fridge with scotch. He knew it was my passion. We drank, and we reminisced for hours. I think the driver drove aimlessly so we could drown our sorrows, which we needed and appreciated. We were on our second bottle of scotch when I began to explain how I had been missing everyone from the group, which prompted Will to ask what happened to Samuel. The fact that he wasn't at the funeral totally eluded me. It got me thinking, why didn't he come? Samuel was never one for saying something and not following through.

I decided to call him from the car phone, but again there was no answer. When I looked at the time, it was past six. He must have been on an outing with his family because I thought one of his kids would have answered otherwise. His kids slept by that damn phone. I understood why he could have changed his mind and not come. It was probably for the same reason I wanted to bail. He wanted to remember her as she was.

The limousine finally found my house. I hugged Vanessa and Will, thanked them, and said I would see them soon.

With great effort, I stumbled to my door and unlocked it and went straight for my bed. I was completely intoxicated and slept until three in the morning.

I woke up with a splitting headache from my binge but managed to get up and shuffle myself to the bathroom. After relieving myself, I opened up the medicine cabinet to get an Aspirin. My head was pounding so hard. I took four pills, washed them down with a glass of water, and headed to the living room. I sat on the couch for over ten minutes with my eyes closed. Praying the pounding would dissipate. I continuously massaged my temples, and slowly the pain subsided to the point where I could concentrate while the pills took their effect.

I decided to head to the kitchen and make myself a bowl of cereal. Cheerios were the only cereal I ate. I remember my mom always trying to get me to eat others, but I was stubborn. I poured a glass of juice for myself and took it along with my cereal to the living room. My headache by that time had completely subsided. I just sat on the couch, finishing my breakfast and watching a family guy rerun. I remember laughing at Peter's antics, trying to play golf instead of celebrating his anniversary with Lois. Found out what Peter was up to, but then the show got interrupted by a news broadcast.

I gathered my dishes and took them to the kitchen. When I walked back into the living room, the broadcast was announcing a plane crash just outside of the city. They had no definitive proof at the time as to what took place but the suspicions of a pilot going berserk. All they could tell us was that 83 people died and no survivors. I, at that point, began to feel really ill. All I could think was Samuel and how I needed to hear his voice. I recall walking toward the phone, so I could call his house, but I passed out and dropped to the floor.

I was awoken again by Will and Vanessa screaming at me to please wake up. They were genuinely worried that I might have been dead. So they kicked in my door when they saw I collapsed. Will helped me up. Vanessa grabbed a chair and pushed it toward me. They asked what was going on, but I just blamed it on some news broadcast I saw. Vanessa then proceeded to ask me if it was about the plane crash. It was, I told her, and then asked how she knew. Will pulled the chair up close and sat down. He looked me right in the eye and asked what upset me so greatly that caused me to pass out. He told me to try and remember what I was thinking just before I collapsed. I recall what ran through my mind, but I didn't want to believe it. I began repeating it wasn't possible; I helped him. I said it wasn't possible; I helped them. Vanessa started crying and hugged me tightly. I just cried with her, embracing her right back. Will's hand rested on my shoulder, squeezing in five-second intervals. I pulled away from Vanessa and asked if either of them had been in contact with his wife. Vanessa had called already and gave her condolences. Ms. Adams said she would phone Vanessa with the details for the funeral.

I recall at that point feeling angry. What good was I doing with these patients of mine if I didn't help Jasmine? She might never have reunited with her father and with Samuel if I had never intervened he might have just quit flying due to the stress. I took that stress away from him so he could fly again.

I got up and asked Will and Vanessa to follow me downstairs because I needed a drink. I decided to crack open the scotch, mainly because it was Samuel's and my favorite. I filled the glasses full to show I wasn't kidding around. We were there to get drunk. Vanessa laughed nervously as she picked up her glass off the table. "To Jasmine and Samuel," I toasted. "May we be able to dream of them in heaven and one day see them again."

We clinked our glasses, and I downed the whole glass of scotch. I emptied the glass completely, pulled it away from my mouth, and said, "That one was for you, old friend," meaning Samuel. The rest of the night went pretty much the same, with us drinking and reminiscing about our deceased comrades.

I actually lost a game of pool to Vanessa. I had never played her before and had no idea how good she was with the stick and those balls. After beating me, she explained she had a lot of practice when she bartended at the pool hall for nearly six years. She was a kid when she worked there, but she hadn't forgotten a thing. In my defense, I was extremely intoxicated and saw three different Wills at the same time that night.

I was so lucky to have friends like Will and Vanessa. They stayed with me the entire night, ensuring I would be okay.

For the next few days, they both kept tabs on me, making sure everything was going smooth and that I wasn't passing out like they experienced the other day.

Wednesday arrived, and again we all had to prepare for the funeral. I felt nervous about going because his family was going to be there. To have to see the children suffering was nothing I wanted to experience. The pain I inadvertently caused them haunted my soul. I hoped that no one else viewed Samuel's tragedy the way I did.

Will had phoned and told me the limo would be arriving soon. I, like last time, put on my best and only suit and walk through the driveway, awaiting my ride.

I stood there for ten minutes, waiting for them. I was relieved because I had no idea what I was going to say or how I would act, or if they would even welcome me there.

The limo turned the corner, and I felt my blood pressure rise. The limo pulled up, and the door opened. To my surprise, it was Mrs. Adams with Will and Vanessa. Mrs. Adams made a judgment call and decided to keep her children at home. When I saw it was her, I felt myself gulp and proceeded to pay my condolences.

Entering the limo, I felt compelled to embrace her and began to weep to plead with her to forgive me. With her hands under my chin, Ms. Adams raised my head to stare into my eyes. She then said that I didn't control fate, and there was nothing I did that warranted the guilt I was feeling. She continued by explaining that since Samuel had met me, he had never been happier. I thought I would feel better when Mrs. Adams released me from the guilt I was harnessing. But I was wrong. I missed my friend.

The funeral was just for close friends and family. I felt honored I was allowed to attend. Everyone that came wrote a poem or a song. One person just got up there and spoke from his heart.

After everyone had recited their poems, I decided to speak. I had nothing planned, so I just talked about his wardrobe. One thing he loved was his fine tailored clothes. I made a joke about when I first saw him that he looked like some 1950s detective and just ended up with how much I was going to miss his quick wit. I finished my humble speech and stepped down.

The preacher said the last words, and the funeral ended. I stayed back because I wanted to say a prayer in private. But while standing there, I began to get dizzy and had to go down to one knee while I tried to fight it off. I had flashes of darkness like I was about to lose consciousness. The episodes had been happening so frequently that I was beginning to learn how to fight through most of them.

A few minutes passed, and the feeling subsided. I got up and walked to the limo, trying to conceal that I had just experienced another blackout.

On the ride home, I was confused as to why I was still experiencing the blackouts when we had stopped the experiments. I was hoping they would eventually stop, but they just seemed to get worse. I knew it was time to let Will know how severe they had become and knew how angry he would be. But I never thought he would punch me.

Chapter Eighteen

A week had passed since the funeral, and I had been dodging Will's phone calls. When he did catch me, I told him I was busy with work, and I would call him. I intended to call him; I just wasn't sure how I would bring up the topic concerning my blackouts.

When I phoned him, he sounded hurt by my actions over the past week. He tried to rush me off the phone, but I was completely honest and told him it was an important issue we needed to discuss. When he heard the tone of my voice, all of our petty problems disappeared, and he dropped everything he was doing and came right over.

I invited him in. We went downstairs, poured him a drink and began explaining my actions since the experiment began. When I told him the blackouts began intensifying the same time we started the experiment, Will leaned into me and slugged me right in the face. He knocked me right off my chair, stood up, and told me I was the most irresponsible doctor he had ever met. He was puzzled as to why I put everyone at risk. He continued by saying that I had a death wish and if I wanted to kill myself, to do it alone and not take anyone with me. He was extremely upset with me but managed to help me off the floor and then apologized. When he realized I had enough, Will began damage control and reminded me of our friendship and how he couldn't bear to lose another friend. He was right, and I knew it. I pretty much had enough anyway and had already decided the blackouts were becoming a problem. Will calmed himself, and he and I sat back and talked as we killed another bottle of whiskey. For the whole night, whenever there was a silent moment, he would fill it with angry insults. For instance, telling me, I was an idiot. His comments didn't faze me. I deserved everything he said, and I knew it.

Six in the evening rolled around. Will mentioned he had to pick up Vanessa from the zoo. She planned a birthday party for her niece and all of her friends, which in my opinion, was quite courageous. Children to me were just dirty, mucus, spewing little people with the attention span of a fruit fly. It just grossed me out.

I walked to the door to see him off. Just before he left, he urged me to call him if any blackouts occurred. He took my hand, squeezed it and pulled me close. Then, with conviction, he reminded me that day or night, he was there for me. Then let my hand free and walked to his car. Will never disappointed or failed to do the right thing since I met him, so I knew he was the right person to have on my side when dealing with the blackouts.

I decided to take a shower. A shower, for some reason, always rejuvenated me, and I felt I was running on empty. I couldn't believe that two friends I held so dear were gone. And the experiment that was supposed to launch my career was scrapped. Not to mention the seizures I had now somehow acquired were slowly chipping away at my sanity. It was not a good year, to say the least. After showering, I got dressed and decided to leave the house. The last thing I needed was to add isolation to the list. So I got in my car and went to visit my parents.

I needed another one of my mother's pep talks. No matter the situation, she always knew what to say to cheer me up somehow. The one thing I loved best about my mom was her sense of humor. It was her timing that made her hilarious. She conjured up such witty comments to make me smile even when I was upset with her. It was a gift that I never took for granted and also what made me the person I am today. Her view on life was so simplistic. She once told me that if you can't laugh at yourself when you mess up, somewhere in your life, you lost sight of what was important. And there was more than enough madness in the world without us adding to it. My mom was by far the most off-the-wall person I had ever encountered. But when you weed through the irrelevant gibberish, you would see the genius hiding between the rants.

I arrived at my parents' close to eight in the evening. My dad was attending his weekly bowling league, and my mother was in the kitchen baking apple crisps. It was amazing how well they got along. I love my dad, but not many women could handle his archaic way of thinking. But he found my mom, who wanted nothing more than to please all of us. They were truly a match made in heaven.

The moment I walked in and smelled the apple crisp, I knew my dad was bowling. My parents have been repeating this routine for as long as I can remember. When I was a child, I used to try to convince my dad to go bowling just so my mom would make apple crisp. He understood my motivation after a while, and my mom began saving a portion just for me. It worked too. When I realized I could get apple crisp without my dad having to bowl, I stopped pressuring him.

My mom was surprised when I walked in. Her arms opened as soon as she saw me and rushed toward me. She knew what I had been through and wanted nothing more than to ease my pain. She and I stood there for several minutes, sharing an embrace. There was nothing anyone could say that would take away the sorrow I felt. And somehow, she knew it. All I needed was to be hugged and told everything would be fine, which was exactly what she did.

When I regained my composure, she told me to sit at the table, and she cut me out a huge piece of apple crisp and topped it off with two scoops of chocolate ice cream. While I scarfed down my dessert, she asked how work was going. I told her I decided to take a sabbatical for the sole purpose of healing, plus it would have been irresponsible to take on anyone if I was unable to offer up a complete concentration.

She agreed with me and quickly changed the subject by asking how I like the apple crisp.

10:30 rolled around when I decided to leave for home. I was hoping to see my dad that night, but he was running late. My mom and I both knew he must have won because that was the only time he was ever late. They would head to the bar whenever they won, and he would come back all excited and happy, which was a sight to see only because he was a master at containing his emotion except when he went bowling. My mom and I used to laugh at him uncontrollably when I was a kid.

I got home, collapsed on the sofa and turned on the TV. I recall watching some French movie with English subtitles. I couldn't speak French, and the film was god awful. When I first tuned in, I caught a glimpse of a woman's breasts, so I kept watching, hoping to see her again.

During the movie, my phone kept ringing, but I felt so exhausted I refused to answer. Whoever it was should have checked the time and realized how inappropriate it was to be phoning after midnight. I just lay there listening to the movie, not understanding a word. I had given up on reading the subtitles due to the movie sucking. Hoping to see some nudity, I fought to stay awake but eventually fell victim to the sandman.

I remember it was close to four in the morning when I heard someone banging ferociously at my door and continuously chiming the bell. To be honest, I was terrified beyond belief but found the courage to rise from the sofa and gingerly shuffled over to the door. The knocking subsided as I approached. I looked out the spy hole, and to my surprise, it was Will standing there. I was about to let him in when he began banging again, telling me to wake up. I couldn't understand why he was at my doorstep at that ungodly hour but knew I had to let him in. He wouldn't have been there unless it was serious, so I unlocked the door.

When I opened it, Will pushed himself in and seemed to be furious at first. All he uttered was it was my fault and pushed me to the ground. He kicked me, screaming how I could have been so reckless. I was curled up in a fetal position, protecting myself from his uncontrollable rage, pleading with him to stop and tell me what I did. I finally got through to him, or he just ran out of strength, I'm not sure which. But when he did stop, Will fell to his knees, covered his face with his hands, and began to sob hysterically. Still crying from my wounds, I managed to sit up and move closer to him. I wasn't sure at the time if he was done kicking my ass, but he was obviously hurting, and I wanted to help him. Very concerned with his wellbeing, I asked him to talk to me and explain what had happened. I sat there beside him, waiting for a response. It took him a second to stop crying before he could raise his head. Will just stared at me in silence with this lifeless expression on his face. He wiped the tears from his eyes, and with all the strength he could muster, still fighting to hold back tears, managed to tell me in a weak, trembling tone that Vanessa was killed that day.

Instead of feeling sorrow for what had transpired, fear shot through my entire body. I grabbed Will by the shoulder and shook him, exclaiming he tell me how she died. I had to scream at him a few times before he finally cried out that she fell into the wolf den at the zoo and she was torn apart. He said it was a freak accident with a hot dog cart.

A group of teenagers were referring a football around on the walkway, and one of them ran into the cart, which sent it barreling into Vanessa and caused her to fall in with the wild animals, Will explained. By the time anyone could get to her, she was mangled, and the only reason he knew was he had to go to the morgue and somehow identify those remains.

I couldn't bear to look him in the eyes. This was my fault, and we both knew it. Staring at the tiles on the floor, I begged him to forgive me and acknowledged that it was my doing. Somehow this was on me, but I had no idea how. I asked Will how what happened could have happened. How could this be possible? There was no way our night terrors could be coming true. It made no sense. Yet, it was hard to dismiss the death of three of our dearest friends who were now gone.

I again pleaded with Will to forgive me, then continued explaining that if this was happening, there were still four people at risk: Jamal, Karen, Richard and, of course, me.

Will gained his composure and stood up with his hand. He gestured to help me out. I latched on to his hand as he lifted me off the floor. He then proceeded to apologize for kicking me in the stomach those thirty times and continued by saying the responsibility was on both of us. We both knew we were experimenting without approval. I immediately stifled all talk concerning who was at fault and urged him to try and focus on how we were going to reverse the process. We headed downstairs to the machine.

The first thing we needed was to check the data Will had acquired. He and I tirelessly sifted through everything for hours with nothing to show for it. Will then asked if he could see the journal I had been writing in since we launched the experiment and kept it upstairs in what was going to become my office so I could also do work at home. But it just became a gigantic file cabinet. Every time I entered that room, I felt like Russell Crowe in *A Beautiful Mind.* To anyone else, it would look strange and somewhat unsettling, but I truly found a place for every item there, so I could find it easier.

I ran to the office, and the bottom right-hand drawer was exactly where I had left it.

I scampered downstairs and handed my journal to Will. While he browsed the book, I went to the bar and pulled the two glasses off the shelf. I recall searching everywhere for the whiskey. Then the rum came up empty. We had a choice, with only vodka or tequila, but tequila always knocked me on my ass. So I played it safe and poured us vodka and orange on rocks. I think I must have been a bartender in a previous life because mixing drinks was always a passion. I was quite good.

I brought the drinks to the table and placed Will's down next to him. He had scanned through most of the journal and seemed to be reading something important because he couldn't look away. I sat there in silence for nearly five minutes, sipping my drink and watching Will's eyes move back and forth as he read all my innermost thoughts as naked as I felt. The urge to find some correlation between the death of our friends and our dreams failed in comparison. Will finished reading the page he was on and then asked what I meant when I said it felt like we weren't supposed to remember. And another page, I wrote that it felt like something was trying to prevent us from remembering, so we would have to concentrate harder next time. I recall my quote the moment he read it. Also, how difficult it was to stay coherent when we were running the experiment.

I began to explain to Will that when the group and I were together in the dream state, trying to remember where we were was a constant struggle, but eventually, we all perfected it. I went on to explain that working with the second group was so much easier just because my experience from the first group educated me on the concentration level we needed to attain to stay together successfully. Will seemed puzzled as to why. At first, it was difficult for us to grasp the concept of actually being coherent well in a different consciousness, but we felt confident we were onto something. Will then ask if I wanted to take a ride. He was sure that a friend of his would be able to help. Her name was Serena Gomez, and she had been like a second mother to Will growing up. He hadn't talked to her for years, but he felt it was time for a visit.

On the way there, Will explained to me that she was a psychic and that she could possibly help us. When he told me she was psychic, I thought it would be a waste of time and demanded we stay focused. I thought it was only a matter of time before I was next. The first group was dead except for me, and if I didn't save myself, then the rest of my patients would surely perish. Will reiterated the meeting with Serena was the right course of action, and if anyone could give us an explanation, it would be her. The one thing my parents taught me was to keep an open mind, so I guess we had to go.

It took a couple of hours, but we finally arrived. Serena's house was modest and very tidy. He trotted up the sidewalk, and I glanced around, observing the flowers bordering her entire yard and the biggest bird bath I had ever set my eyes on. It was working too. I swear there were ten birds sipping and frolicking of all different species. It was a beautiful sight.

We approached the door, and Will gave it a pound. As we stood there, we heard an old female voice scream for us to wait. Due to her not being as young as she used to be, Serena opened the door and, looking at Will, began to scream. She lunged toward him and squeezed him tight, repeating how much she had missed him. After prying himself away from Serena, she invited us in. Walking into her house, instantly, my mood changed. I saw rabbit's feet, a monkey's paw, stuffed cats, and even a skull placed right in the middle of the kitchen table.

My skepticism returned, and again I felt we were wasting our time. Just then, the most interesting thing happened. She turned to me and assured us that everything that breaks could be fixed. I don't know why, but her comment calmed me. She just blurted it out with no subtext but knew we needed guidance immediately.

I agreed with Will we were in the right place.

Chapter Nineteen

Will and I sat at the table. As she sat down, she introduced herself.

"My name is Serena Gomez," she said.

She continued telling us that she had been practicing her psychic abilities since she was a young child. She told us that the first time she knew she was gifted was when a dream of hers came true. She dreamt that she was riding the bus, and out the window, a friend of hers from school got hit by a car. The boy was trying to cross the street when he walked out from in front of the bus and was crushed. Two days after her dream, the event came true. From that point on, she would write her dreams down. Since then, she has harnessed her ability and was able to tune it in and out.

Serena stood up, apologized for her manners, and offered us tea. While she was making it, she asked what we needed from her and how it had to do with dreams. I began to explain my experiment and how it was meant to curb night terrors. She was intrigued, to say the least. I told her how I had already cured six people with the help of hypnotism. Serena stopped me and asked how I could possibly know for sure I cured them. At first, she thought I had found a way to suppress their dreams, but when I explained I was in there with them, it confused her further. That was when I told her about the machine Will and I created and its function. I continued explaining how a sleep inducer would be introduced once I had them under hypnosis, which enabled me to link up with them in their dreams.

Serena placed our tea on the table and sat back down. While I talked, her facial expressions turned very serious. She listened intently as I told her how I helped patients not only curb their night terrors but also eliminate the fear that followed, which initially caused their problems. Serena interrupted and looked concerned with a frightened glare. She exclaimed to Will and I that we had no idea what we were toying with and warned us that we were not just fooling with people's dreams; we were meddling with spirits from different dimensions. "It's like a waiting room," she said, "for our spirits while we sleep. But amongst our spirits are also lost and confused spirits, trying to find a place to go. The one thing the lost spirits are drawn to is our life force. And that is where our dreams come from. When we sleep, these entities surround us, trying to convince us that we should take them with us when we awake. For the most part, we can fight them off, but some get angry and threaten to hurt us just for the possibility they might escape."

The next thing she said terrified me because they finally understood what I had done. Serena said that the only thing preventing spirits from entering our world is our fear. The fear that we remember when we wake up is what actually keeps them contained in their world. It's a defense mechanism equivalent to an electromagnetic pulse. The more terrifying the dream, the closer the spirits are to entering our world. When we die in our dreams, it means spirits are latched on, and the fear we experience creates an energy force around us so great that it would force all unwanted entities away from us, the living, as we slip back into our bodies. "If you take that away," Serena continued, "you leave an open doorway for anything to pass through. And the moment your patients seize to experience fear is when the door opens, and it will remain open until their fear is returned."

Will and I stared at each other, realizing our catastrophic blunder. I looked back at Serena and asked if anyone could die from my experiment. All she could tell me was that whatever was done needed to be undone. If a door to another dimension is left open, it will eventually find a way to close. She ended by saying that death would be a definite way to close the door.

Serena stood up, told us that's all she could help us with and walked us to the door.

Just before we left, she took my hand, closed her eyes, and stood there. I waited a good minute before it got uncomfortable. I turned toward Will and motioned for him to do something. But just then, Serena lifted her head. She felt she had to warn me that the spirits were strong around me, and they felt angry. She then told me that I was not in danger, but everyone around me was unless I found a way to calm them. She warned me that whatever I did created a link between me and another dimension with which I had no business tampering. The spirits don't want me, she reiterated. They want the people I brought with me. She finished by explaining that for some reason, the spirits were telling her that I was there but not there. And they didn't like the fact that I was in and out. I was confused by what she had said and asked what it meant, but she had no idea. She was just the messenger, she replied and asked us to leave.

Will and I got back into his car, discussing our next move. We decided to see the remaining group and try to figure out what to do. I was terrified that whatever I released was skipping me and was going after the rest of them. I concluded that I wasn't affected by this unknown entity because I wasn't hypnotized. Since the group was under my control while we were asleep, they were compelled to listen to just my voice. I had taught them how not to fear, which was now obvious. I had to teach them how to fear again. I actually needed to terrify my patients, which was ironic if you think about it. I tried to save them by helping curb their night terrors. Now, the only way to save them was to give those night terrors right back. When I expressed my feelings to Will, for a moment, we laughed, which eased the tension we were feeling.

Will and I decided to see Jamal first since he was the most afraid and the closest. I didn't know how I would tell

Jamal of all the people that his life was in danger and he could possibly die the same way he would have in his dream. The terror I saw in his eyes when it was only a dream was bad enough, but this needed to be done.

I remember pulling up to the front of Jamal's place, unsure how I would approach him. I told Will I wanted to figure out what I was going to say to break the news.

Before we went up, we sat in the car for close to fifteen minutes. Just silent. I looked at Will, took a deep breath, and opened the car door. Will followed suit and got out. We shut the doors. I slammed my hands down on the car's roof and exclaimed to Will that I knew how we would do it. We would tell him everything was fine, but we needed to run a couple more tests to ensure everything was running smoothly. I didn't see why we needed to tell him the truth, especially if we could rectify this situation. Will agreed that it was a good course of action.

We had a plan and proceeded toward his apartment block. Will and I didn't take more than three steps toward the building when a huge explosion happened; the blast knocked me back ten feet, landing on the sidewalk. I recall being dizzy but quickly shook it off. I stood up dumbfounded and watched the flames porter off the bottom floor of the windows. Frantically, I called out to Will with a pitiful yelp. Will cried out that he was alright; the blast knocked him back and slammed him into the car door. I limped toward him and helped him up. Will and I just stood there watching Jamal's apartment burn out of control. We had no idea how the explosion happened, but new Jamal was in there. Will and I watched the blaze burn out of control. At the same time, we were mesmerized by its immense power.

The fire truck quickly arrived. Firefighters pulled out the hoses and promptly attached them to the fire hydrants. As the water danced with the fire, pushing it back, a crowd began to form tirelessly. The firefighters battled this gigantic flame, trying to keep it from getting out of control. Nearly half an hour passed when everyone watching was compelled to flee due to the loud breaking noise. Then, without warning, the building came crashing down, leaving nothing but rubble and a roaring fire. The smoke by that time got too thick to breathe. That's when the firefighters asked the remaining few to evacuate from the area.

Will and I jumped back into the car and drove off, watching the fire blaze in the rearview mirror, knowing Jamal was just buried alive. I suggested to Will that we stay together until we figured out where the others were, so we returned to my place.

I ran downstairs, snagged the bottle of vodka from behind the bar, and quickly ran it back up so Will and I could calm our nerves.

We sat in the kitchen, sipping our drinks, frantically trying to contact Karen and Richard. I left numerous messages but had yet to hear back from either, which caused Will and I to worry that much worse. The last thing I wanted was to make orphans out of Richard's children. I cared for Karen as well; I just had a special place in my heart for Richard and his little ones. And I just needed to hear his voice to ensure they were safe. I phoned repeatedly, and when I couldn't do it anymore, Will tried.

Hours went by with Will and I phoning, drinking, and phoning. We became so inebriated that as soon as I put down the phone, Will would pick it up again and try it. We both, after a while, were just acting foolish. Plus, some of our messages probably made little to no sense. Will was intoxicated and ready to pass out. I was not far behind. The vodka bottle was close to empty, so I shot the rest back. I finished it quickly and slammed it down on the counter like I had just accomplished something. I even remember smiling, then looking at Will, acknowledging that the bottle was empty.

Just then, the phone began screaming, making both Will And I jump out of our chairs. We just stared at the phone for a second like we had discovered fire. I was wasted and had to stumble to answer the phone. I managed to lift the receiver and brought it to my ear. Slurring, I asked who was phoning at that ungodly hour like it mattered. It was Karen returning the messages Will and I had left, which seemed to have annoyed her. She didn't appreciate us phoning while we were intoxicated and told me to phone her in the morning when I had some sense. I agreed that I was out of line and apologized, but I told her we needed to talk at that very moment. Fumbling with what I needed to say didn't sit well with Karen, but I insisted she listened. I must have said 'listen' a dozen times, trying to explain her life was in danger, but my slurring and pleading with her to listen was not convincing.

The next thing I know, a powerful jolt shot up my spine, right to my head. I recall screaming and dropping the phone to cradle my head with my hands. Will rushed over and asked if I was alright. I was not; everything was going dark as I felt myself blacking out. The pain I was feeling in my head was new and unpleasant, which was the last thing I remembered until I woke. I opened my eyes to see Will and Karen hovering over me, genuinely concerned that I might have died again, but they were both overwhelmed when I began to move. They still looked concerned, so I tried to reassure them that everything was fine and that we had worse things on our plate. I abruptly changed the subject and asked if anyone got in touch with Richard, but they hadn't, which concerned all of us.

While I was unconscious, Will explained to Karen what we thought was happening and that we wanted her to remain with us until we found a way to stop whatever it was that was after her and Richard. I apologized to Karen for all the messages we had left and the mess I got them into. I never had any intention of making their problems worse. Karen was alarmed but was dealing. She accepted my apology and replied that under the circumstances, she completely understood why we were drinking and then asked if she could partake.

"By all means," I stated, but the catch was that she had to go to the basement and get it. We were just too drunk. "Grab whatever was down there," I told her, which I think was only tequila. I suggested she bring the entire arsenal because we would need it, which prompted us to bellow out in a nervous chuckle as Karen proceeded to the basement.

While she was down there, I asked Will what he said to Karen and if I needed to know anything. He was as honest with her as he could be. He told her that we needed to get her back into the machine because we inadvertently opened something in her subconscious that we needed to shut before something bad happened to her. We then reassured her that everything would be fine because she was safe with us. We would perform the experiment one last time and reverse the process. I was so appreciative to have Will in my corner because I was still so rattled. I could have probably made the situation worse.

Will always seemed to be in control like nothing fazed him. I think he had been working on computers for a long time and was now capable of acting like one. He rarely exuded any emotion.

The phone rang during Will and my conversation; it was Richard phoning back. He was laughing when I answered. I greeted him and asked if everything was okay. He said he was fine but then asked what we were doing, pranking him in the middle of the night. He wasn't upset. If anything, he thought we were hilarious but begged me not to attempt it again because children might wake up next time, which would not be as funny. I apologized for being an idiot and then continued explaining that the phone calls were supposed to be a warning that he might be in danger but turned into the world's dumbest pranksters. I explained that he needed to get a babysitter and get over to my house as soon as possible because we needed to get him back into the machine one last time. I told him I had opened something in their dreams that shouldn't have been tampered with, and we needed to move as quickly as possible. I cared for Richard, so I told him the severity of the situation and how many of my patients had died due to this matter and in which they perished. He thought I was kidding at first and told me to go to hell, laughing it off, which encouraged me to raise my voice and urge him to get his ass to my house immediately. He knew then I was serious and told me he would be there soon.

I hung up the phone and stared at Will, hoping we weren't too late. He reassured me that everything was going to be fine. I recall saying that I hoped we reached them in time when, out of nowhere, a tremendous crash came from the basement, immediately following a scream from Karen to please help her. I thought because Karen was with us, she was safe.

When Will and I got to the basement, I realized they were not safe anywhere.

Chapter Twenty

Will and I scurried to the basement to find that one of the deprivation chambers toppled over and ripped the hose out of the wall where the water flowed and now was spewing everywhere. I looked around to find Karen but couldn't pinpoint her until she let out this fantastic scream.

When the chamber fell over, it somehow rolled on Karen's legs, and she was pinned to the floor. When I asked how it happened, she told me she heard a weird noise, so she went to investigate. By the time she realized what was happening, the hose had ripped from the wall, and the chamber rolled off its braces and pinned her. I asked if her legs were broken and if she could move, to which her response was she was fine, just needed us to move the chamber.

Will grabbed one end, and I grasped onto the other. On the count of three, we pulled. I tugged so hard I felt my eyeballs protruding from my sockets. Every muscle I had was straining but to no avail. We were unable to budge it.

The water kept pouring in and rising while frantically I searched around to find something we could use to pry the chamber off of her. I told Will I was looking for some sort of metal rod so we could get under the chamber. Will and I tore my basement apart while Karen repeatedly screamed for us to hurry. The water was rising ferociously. It was at my knees by that time, making it very difficult to move.

Will located a long metal rod and screamed in triumph. We raced over to Karen, sitting up by that time, holding the chamber because the water had risen to her waist. Karen shouted at us to hurry. She could feel the water submerging her elbows and could not sit up any straighter.

We shoved the metal pole under the chamber, and Will pulled with all his might. His face turned bright red when he demanded I get behind him and help. I leaped through the rising water, dropped behind him, and began to pull. My hands were wet. I could feel them slowly slipping. We heaved with all our strength while Karen screamed and Will pleaded to pull harder. I knew my grip wouldn't hold and yelped out that I was losing it. Karen pleaded with me to hang on and hurry, and Will assured me we were close and to keep pulling.

The water had reached Karen's neck and splashed up against her chin when unexpectedly, the metal rod bent, which brought the chamber crashing down on Karen's knees. She cried out, taking in a mouthful of water. Terrified, she quickly spat out the water and began crying hysterically, begging for us to save her while taking on yet another mouthful of water. Will and I were at a loss, but we grabbed the chamber again and tried to move it. We grappled with it, but there was nothing we could do. I looked back at Karen, and she was completely submerged under water. All I could see was her panicking eyes staring back at me, praying we could help her.

Realizing she was close to running out of breath, I dropped to my knees and attempted to feed her my oxygen. Will tirelessly kept pushing on the chamber but knew it was a losing battle. I kept providing Karen oxygen, and she ripped at my hair, trying to save herself. Will stopped pushing, turned around, and dropped, sitting himself down into the rising water. When I asked what was happening, he just stared at me with a blank look on his face. Then burst out crying. I knew then that the battle was over. I screamed at Will to help me; I don't know why. I knew Karen was dying. I gave her one last breath, hoping something would intervene and save her, but it never did.

Karen began to flare her arms under the water, slashing hysterically and all I could do was watch as the light drained from her eyes and slowly drifted away. Karen stopped moving as her lifeless body lay bobbing in the water.

I was reminded of when I first began the experiment and how soothing it was to lay in those chambers, completely engulfed in darkness. Whatever it was, stalking and killing my patients was not getting away with it. For the first time, I felt enraged and was determined to set things right, even if it meant my own life. This was nobody's fault but mine, and my patients did not deserve this.

I turned to Will and regrettably told him that Karen was dead. I then told him to wipe his eyes, suck it up and follow me. We were not waiting for Richard; we were going to him. Will picked his head up, lifted his drenched, aching body from the rising water, and wiped his tears. He pulled himself together, and with a fierce, convincing tone, he was fine and ready for anything. I could tell he was livid and might have just hit his breaking point. It was imperative that Will kept his sanity because he was the only one who knew how to run the chambers. So, I decided to claim full responsibility for Karen. I was the one that created the mess we were in, and I added that he was not the least bit culpable. I then looked him in the eye and reassured him that we would finish this, save Richard and destroy the machine so no one would ever get hurt again.

I splashed through the water toward the stairs, and then Will came up right behind. Just as I was shutting the door, I remember turning around and just staring, watching my basement as it continued to fill up with water. Karen was completely submerged, and I couldn't even see her anymore. I felt such guilt knowing she was dead when suddenly, a surge of adrenaline shot through my body. I turned around, slammed the door, and decided to call Richard again, hoping he was close. Richard answered and said he was on his way but was running late. I decided we weren't waiting. I knew we still had to pick his kids up from daycare, so I suggested we meet downtown. When Richard explained where the daycare was, all I could picture was the size of the building and Richard's recurring dream. I begged Richard to wait outside until we got there, and he and I would go in together. He told me to calm down at first, but I became adamant, so he reluctantly agreed.

Will and I frantically bolted to my car and sped off. I remember racing through the traffic, running red lights, and honking my horn like a crazy person. When I looked over at Will for just a moment, his hands were braced against the dashboard while his eyes were bugging out of his head. I knew he was a little freaked out, but I refused to slow down at the risk of losing Richard. He was the last of them, and I couldn't let him down. Before we knew it, we pulled up to the building, and just as I asked, Richard was waiting outside. I leaped out of the car and pleaded with Richard that he not, under any circumstances, enter that building. I told him I would retrieve his children and bring them to him just as long as he stayed with Will. Richard was dumbfounded but saw the intensity on my face, so he decided to cooperate.

Richard phoned the daycare and explained that he was downstairs, but he would be sending me up. He made up some story about hurting his leg and couldn't walk so it wouldn't appear conspicuous.

I entered the building and proceeded to the elevator. My heart was thumping so loud. At one point, I wondered if the woman beside me waiting for the elevator had heard it. I wasn't sure what would happen but knew Richard would be safe. The fact that I was taking Richard's place probably would prevent anything from happening. I feared that I might have prevented a catastrophic event with Richard that day, but if I couldn't find a way to reverse the process, his night terror would surely become a reality.

The elevator door opened. I let the lady go first, and I followed. I pressed six for myself and asked the woman what floor she needed. She was also going to the sixth floor and thanked me for asking. The elevator felt like it wasn't even moving. While staring at the numbers on the elevator, I noticed I was perspiring profusely. The elevator was moving at such a slow pace it caused me to start panicking. My hands and knees were shaking; sweat was trickling into my eyes. With my hand, I wiped away the sweat beating down my face and took a deep breath. Nervously, I began pressing the number six, praying for the elevator to hurry. The woman beside me decided to start a conversation by telling me that pressing the button won't make the elevator go any quicker and then added that the elevator had always been slow. I let out a nervous giggle, agreed that the elevator was slow, and suggested that someone repair it. She then explained that the elevator was calibrated that way on purpose due to the infants. I appreciated her talking to me; it got my mind off the situation. Before I knew it, the doors opened.

Immediately, I was surrounded by kids and mothers wanting to get into the elevator. Cautiously, I pushed through the crowd looking for an employee when halfway into the classroom, I spotted Richard's offspring and proceeded toward them. When they saw me, they both recognized me and gave me a big giant hug. I stuck with the story and told them their dad was outside waiting because he hurt his foot, which is why I was there instead. Just then, Heather, an employee, introduced herself and asked who I was. I introduced myself, ensured everything was okay and confirmed they received a call from Richard. Everything seemed to go off without a hitch.

The kids and I got into the elevator, left the building, and I handed the little tikes over to Richard.

We all got back into the car, not saying a word. The silence in the vehicle was deafening. I had no idea what to do. My basement was flooded, so the machines were useless to us, and I decided that we would all have to stay together. I informed Richard that something terrible was happening, and I wasn't sure just what to do, so we were all staying with him and his children. Richard became upset and demanded that we come clean about exactly what was happening. I told him to calm down, but he was beyond that point. He insisted that we explain ourselves immediately, or he wanted out of the vehicle. I realized he was frightened and told him to wait until we got to his house and Will and I would reveal everything. I also added that he would not like what he heard, but I owed him the truth.

Chapter Twenty-One

We quickly arrived at Richard's place. When we got inside, Richard told his kids to go upstairs and play so the grown-ups could talk.

Richard, Will, and I sat at the kitchen table, and I was nothing but honest with everything. I needed him to know the severity of the danger he was in. So left nothing out. When I finished, he was astonished at how irresponsible I was and wondered if I ever knew what I was doing. Then he turned to Will and asked how he could have condoned such behavior. I was in no position to defend myself, knowing that everything Richard was saying was accurate. I just sat there and let him reprimand me. Nothing he could say that day would make me feel any worse than I already felt. They were all dead. And it was my fault. Samuel, Karen, and Jamal were all gone. And Jasmine, the only woman that loved me, despite my many flaws, I killed her. Nothing made sense to me anymore. So all I could think when Richard scolded me was to bring it on because I knew I deserved every ridicule.

Richard wanted us to understand that whatever happened, his children needed to be safe. When he pleaded for his children, my heart fell into my stomach. When my eyes overflowed with tears, I assured him that nothing would happen to him, but God forbid he needn't worry. I would take them in, I cried, and not only because of a sense of obligation. I had grown to care for his family, so even if I had never endangered his life and created a scenario that he could possibly die in, in the exact manner he would have in his nightmares, and now we're stalking him, trying to take his life so things would revert to the way it was. Yes, I still would've helped him with his show. My humorous comment sparked a laugh in Richard, which prompted Will and me to burst out howling. The uncontrollable giggle went on for close to a minute when abruptly, everything went silent. After our laugh fest broke the tension, I took the opportunity to offer my sincere apology and hope sometime down the road; he could find a way to forgive me.

What Richard said following my grand speech was exactly why I held him in such high regard, his strong unbreakable character. He just let me off the hook. A gesture I felt unworthy of. He reminded me why I started the experiment in the first place, which was to help people. Nothing I did, he remarked, was intentional or vindictive. He added that I was a complete buffoon going in blind, but my heart was in the right place. Plus, the time for the blame game had come and gone. We needed to figure out how to reverse whatever I had done. That meant we had to return to my place and fix the deprivation chambers.

We devised a plan that as soon as the weekend came, which was only a couple of days away, Richard would pawn his children off to his neighbor, and we would fix those machines for one last adventure. And after that, we would destroy them for good. Richard rose from the table and said he would set up a couple of places for us to bunk. He decided that Jesse and Tomlin, his two kids, would sleep on the pullout in the living room. Will and I could have their room. I was worried we were an inconvenience to Richard and the kids. So I voiced my concerns. There were no problems at all, Richard replied in a joking tone. It turns out Jesse and Tomlin liked nothing more than to crash in the living room. It was like camping, they thought. Plus, when everyone was asleep, they would quietly turn on the TV and pig out on junk. So if anything, they were more than pleased to have us there.

Richard proceeded upstairs, changed the sheets, and fluffed up the pillows. The best part about staying in Tomlin's room was he had UFC for Xbox 360. It was a game I used to play when it first came out. For brief moments that night, playing that game, I recalled all the tragedy I had experienced washed away, even if only for an hour. I cherished every minute.

While Richard was upstairs, fluffing, Will took the time to contact Vanessa's mother. Her parents took care of the funeral arrangements, and Will wanted to offer help in any way he could but was intimidated to make the call. I sat at the table, sipping on coffee I had decided to brew, waiting for Will and Richard to finish their tasks. I had the opportunity to analyze Will's body language while he conversed with Vanessa's mother. It absolutely killed me to see Will choosing every word he uttered so carefully, all the while unable to raise his head from staring at the floor. Even though Carol, Vanessa's mother, was unaware of the events that had transpired, will felt a sense of obligation to covet his guilt, which in my opinion, should have fallen on me. It was my burden, not his; I tried to tell him.

Will ended the phone call and sat there for a while before joining me in the kitchen. From what I observed, he was fighting to keep his tears back. All I could think while watching him was how many people's lives I had altered and the pain I had caused. I know my intentions were admirable initially, but my ego got the better of me. If I had stopped the experiment after experiencing my first blackout, I would never have begun with the second group.

Will finally stood up, straightened his shirt, and came back to the kitchen without saying a word. He pulled up the chair from the table and flopped himself down, followed by a long exhausting sigh. Will and I just sat there in silence for a moment. I could see he was still absorbing the conversation he had had. So to break the ice, I asked if he wanted a coffee. It took him a moment, but he finally looked up at me and nodded, acknowledging he would. As I prepared the cup of coffee, he informed me that the funeral was the following day and he needed to be ready by two. All I could think to say at that moment was we'll be there, which made me feel like a moron; of course, we would be there. As I stirred his coffee, I quietly scolded myself for uttering such a pointless comment.

I turned toward the table with his coffee, placed it gingerly in front of him, and sat back down. Will took a sip, thanked me, and added that it was good, paused for just a second, and asked if he was okay. The only one that knew as much as I concerning the whole ordeal was Will, so if I was barely keeping it together, I could imagine what was running through his mind. He stared at me for a few seconds, then, with a low defeated tone and dead eyes, he uttered that he was far from all right and probably would never be. He added that the objective was still the same, and I could still count on him. I understood what he meant and added that our lives and everyone else's were forever changed. But the best thing we could do for our sanity was to find a way to forgive ourselves. Otherwise, the guilt would manifest in itself and cause more problems. Will agreed we needed to forgive ourselves eventually but was adamant we needed to suffer for a while before that occurred. That made me laugh. Will smiled for a moment, but he quickly retracted and took another sip of his coffee.

Richard finished making the beds and informed us that we could make ourselves comfortable. Will and I were utterly exhausted, so we quickly thanked Richard for his hospitality and rushed to our rooms.

It didn't take me long to fall asleep. After a few games of UFC, I felt completely wiped out. I recall gently settling into the pillow left for me and remember thinking it was so comfortable. I closed my eyes and fell fast asleep.

The next morning came upon us, and there was a stillness in the air with a sense of dread. Another funeral to attend, another friend to get lowered into the dark, cold soil alone, alone, because of the trust they placed in me. I remember feeling saturated with shame at that moment, by what I had done, I began to wonder if it was in bad taste to attend Vanessa's funeral, due to my being the direct result of her passing. I didn't even want to look at Will that day, knowing I would have to see the pain behind his eyes. I felt so unworthy of Will's friendship, but the responsibility he harbored for participating in the experiment was why I think he still remained bonded. With all the effort I could muster, I sat up, tore the covers off, and leaped out of bed. I slowly got dressed, pondering how I was going to react or what I would possibly say to anyone I encountered at the funeral. I wondered how many people Vanessa talked to concerning the experiment, and what would they know?

Dressed and ready to go, I found myself pacing, postponing the inevitable. I paced back and forth for nearly twenty minutes, trying to convince myself everything would be fine, when a knock at the door compelled me to speed up my process.

“Come in,” I said in a polite, hesitant tone. The door opened. Will being the friend he was, made me a coffee.

“You probably need this,” he said, looking at me like I was innocent of any wrongdoing. He blamed me for nothing. And I knew it, which in my opinion, was worse than him hating me. My guilt was consuming my sanity and it was only a matter of time before I was completely batty.

Will asked how I was doing and if I needed anything. I was good, I told him, and responded by asking if I could possibly do anything for him. He said something and proceeded to ask that while attending the funeral, I not leave his side for any reason. The family members he would have to converse with seemed overwhelming for him to do it alone. I was happy to help. I told him I would be his shadow and not to worry.

I took a sip of my coffee and suggested we’d go downstairs and wait for the limo. Will and I sat downstairs for close to twenty minutes, waiting for the limousine to arrive. We were entertained by Richard and his kids playing guitar hero. Richard wanted to attend so he could pay his respects, but at the last minute, his babysitter canceled, so he was unable to. He wasn’t too acquainted with Vanessa, but Richard was a true Christian and seeing his friend suffering from such deep sorrow compelled him to want to be there for us.

When the limousine arrived, Richard embraced us and pleaded with us to take care of each other. Will and I both agreed we would have each other's back, shook Richard's hand, and left for the funeral.

Entering the limousine, the silence was suffocating. I was no help either, and not for the sake of trying, but every time I was compelled to speak, I was overwhelmed with the sensation of shame and embarrassment, so I decided to stay silent.

We entered the cemetery, and immediately a headache similar to previous ones came upon me, felt like a blackout was about to occur. I felt like it was creeping up on me again. I closed my eyes and recalled breathing very slowly while focusing on my finger as I repeatedly tapped it against my inner thigh.

We pulled up to the site, which looked to have a terrific turnout. Will and I exited the limo. And like I promised, I never left his side. The sensation of the blackout quickly subsided. Will and I began shaking hands with aunts, uncles, cousins, and friends while dodging Vanessa's parents. I felt it immediately because they were in clear view of us at all times, but Will kept his back to them for most of the socializing. Out of the corner of my eye, I observed Vanessa's parents making it over to Will. Casually, I leaned into Will and subtly whispered in his ear that Vanessa's parents were approaching from his six, and he should brace himself. It was a few minutes before they caught up. But when they did, it went better than either of us hoped. All that was exchanged was love, apologies, and hopes that Will would still be a part of their lives even though Vanessa had passed. My heart broke when I heard them say that to Will; it struck Will worse. He immediately began to sob and embrace Vanessa's mom. After a long heartfelt embrace, Will reassured them he was their new adopted son, and they would never get rid of him, which propelled us all to laugh, followed by a moment of silence. I perked up and suggested we head toward our seats, and quickly the crowd began to move.

Walking toward the burial site, I again felt the damn headache creeping up. When I finally approached the coffin and peeked in, the headache, a light throbbing, turned into a ferocious pounding drum that literally hurt my ears with every bang. I attempted to conceal the immense pain I was enduring, but Will picked up on it immediately. He leaned into me and asked what was going on and if I was okay. I told him my head was pounding, but nothing that he needed to concern himself with. I knew I was lying, but I was not taking the attention away from Vanessa and her family. I had intervened and destroyed that family enough. They deserved to have a perfect ceremony, and I intended to give them at least that.

We were all seated, and the priest began the sermon. My head was on fire by that time, but I just bowed my head and meditated, which due to the setting, looked completely normal. I kept the pose for ten minutes, listening to the priest as he spoke about the wonderful things Vanessa had accomplished before her passing. My eyes were still closed, my head screaming. The priest introduced Vanessa's mother. During her speech, I noticed her voice became faint and muffled and no matter how hard I tried, making out anything she said was nearly impossible. I knew I was in trouble, and it was only a matter of time before I collapsed. Nothing about what I was experiencing felt familiar anymore. I experienced these blackouts consistently for some time, and as soon as the headache crept up, it wasn't long before I would pass out. But this time, I stayed awake. Wide awake. I sat there concentrating, trying to control the pain, when the throbbing stopped abruptly. I was unsure at first, so I sat there with my eyes still shut, waiting for the next bolt of lightning to strike my cranium, when I realized that not only did the pain subside, I didn't hear anything. I swiftly opened my eyes to find myself sitting alone on the grass in the middle of the cemetery. Everything was gone. Will, Vanessa, the coffin – gone. Terror immediately engulfed every part of my being. I sprung from the ground and screamed for Will to answer me. With no response, I began pleading for everyone to explain what was happening, with no luck.

I frantically began racing through the cemetery, trying to locate an exit. I hysterically searched the entire cemetery but could not find a gate. Plus, a gigantic wall bordered the entire cemetery, which made it impossible to scale. I felt completely defeated. I prompted myself back down against the enormous headstone and closed my eyes. I have no recollection of how, but when my eyes opened, I found myself again laying on the ground in the middle of the funeral. Will, and Frank, Vanessa's father, were kneeling over me, screaming for me to come to. Ensuring me I was okay and to wake up.

"Wake up," he shouted. "Wake up."

I finally became coherent and sat up. Will helped me to my feet, and I asked if everything was okay. They said, are you okay? And if I needed anything. I reassured him I was fine, apologized to the family for the spectacle I had made, and humbly sat back down.

Embarrassed as hell, I sat there as Frank read his eulogy. He talked about Vanessa for close to ten minutes, not holding back one tear. He was so proud and had such high aspirations for her. He spoke so elegantly. He ended his speech with the Lord's prayer and stepped down. The priest stood up, shook Frank's hand, complimented him on his heartfelt words, then began his closing statements. The priest was nearly finished when the most severe pain I had ever experienced shot from my spine up to my brain stem. All I could recall was letting out an excruciating yell and falling off my chair as I crashed to the ground.

Chapter Twenty-Two

Once again, I woke up alone. Leaning up against the same gravestone I recall leaning on the last time I passed out. This time, one thing was different. In the distance, I saw the funeral I was attending. I had no idea how I wandered off so far from the group, but apparently, I did, and from what I observed, everyone was leaving. Will and I were supposed to have each other's back, but somehow he let me get away. I stood up and proceeded toward the limousine. Will was already there, but the limo drove away before I could reach it. I sprinted after them, screaming for them to stop, but they could not hear me. My yelps were pointless, and I missed my ride.

I looked back at the funeral site, hoping I would hitch a ride with someone else from the group, but no one else was willing to stop. I watched this last limo drive out of the cemetery, and again, I was alone. This time, I was standing by the exit, prompting me to immediately sprint toward it, fearing that something might happen, like it would disappear. I reached the gate of the cemetery. I looked down at the long road in front of me and knew I had a very long journey ahead. I was absolutely livid. For Will to have left me there like he did spoke volumes.

Walking down the long, never-ending piece of concrete gave me ample time to think, which made me realize that this was Will's passive-aggressive way of telling me that he was done with me and blamed me for everything. He had every right to be angry with me and to terminate our friendship, but to leave me at the cemetery, in my opinion, was childish and just plain nasty.

It took me over an hour, but I finally got to the end of that long highway. I was still close to half a mile away, but I saw what looked like a gas station in the distance, which compelled me to pick up my pace. I started a steady jog knowing that the end of this miserable morning was nearly behind me. I reached the station, and to my surprise, a taxi was conveniently filling its tank. My first thought was somebody up in heaven was watching out for me because my luck felt like it had just changed. I approached the cab and pleaded with him to drive me home. I explained my entire morning to him, and he was more than happy to do anything he could. I enthusiastically leaped in the back of the car, feeling extremely relieved. I recall feeling so exhausted I closed my eyes for what seemed like just a moment, but when my eyes again opened, we had already left the gas station, and we were on our way. I immediately felt reassurance that I was in good hands, so again, I closed my eyes and rested.

I abruptly awakened from sleep due to the cabbie slamming on his brakes, realizing he was not going to make a yellow light. I was ready to respond to his poor driving when I realized it was night outside. He must've been driving for close to ten hours. This guy was an absolute lunatic. But when I noticed we were close to my house, I decided not to say anything. I just wanted to get home. We turned onto my street, which was completely congested with police cars, ambulances, and even a goddamn fire truck. I didn't know what was happening, but for some reason, I knew it was my doing. I thought they must've found Karen's body submerged in the basement. There was no way the taxi was getting any closer to my house, so I told him I was good from there. The cabbie told me that the ride was on him and to take care.

"You think so?" I responded in a sarcastic tone, implying that he wasn't getting a cent off me because it took him half the day to locate my house.

I jumped out of the cab, and before I sped off, he told me to take care and sleep tight, laughing hysterically as he drove away. I appreciated the ride, but that taxi was touched in the head. My thought was, if he was lost for so long, why wouldn't he wake me?

I proceeded through the debris of vehicles when it dawned on me that I never told that cabbie my address, nor did he ask. How the hell did he know where to go at all? I thought. Did he know me? That was quite unsettling.

I approached my house and noticed my front door open and police officers trampling on my lawn and all around the house. I froze for a moment, rationalizing the consequences.

If I just turned around and ran, everything would be okay. I decided that things were so out of control I just needed to walk into the house and face whatever was coming. I never intended to hurt anyone, but so many lives were affected. If I didn't own up, then knowing would eventually destroy me anyway. I forced myself, step by step, toward the threshold of my house, slowly, trying not to draw suspicion onto myself. I reached the sidewalk and proceeded toward the door. As I reached the threshold, I peeked, hoping not to be seen. I pushed the door all the way open and walked in. My house was packed with police officers and firefighters, but they did not notice me. Calmly, I walked to the basement door and proceeded down the stairs. I had made it halfway down when I realized the water that once flooded my house had receded. My first thought was they found Karen and were, without a doubt looking for me. I quietly crept down the stairs when I heard screaming. It was Will. I would recognize his yelp anywhere. I leaped down the remaining steps and saw Will at the machine's controls, screaming while police officers frantically tried to open one of the chambers. I don't know how Will did it, but he somehow got the machines hooked up and working again.

I sprinted toward Will and screamed out his name. I asked what he was doing, but all he uttered was to get the damn chambers to open. I turned toward the chamber and frantically began helping the officers. While we attempted to pry open the chamber, I realized Will must've decided to go ahead with the experiment and help Richard by himself, but something obviously went horribly wrong, and Richard was now stuck in the chamber.

Finally, the chamber cracked open a bit, and we could now get our crowbars wedged enough where we could pop the top off. Before we attempted to try to lift the lid, an overwhelming stench of burning flesh filled the room. Will smelled it and screamed out my name. Immediately, I hurried as fast as I could to open the chamber. And with one strong push down on the crowbar, the chamber's top opened. First, all we could see was smoke bellowing from the pod. We knew he was dead. Will was behind me, looking in, and began to cry. All he could do was apologize to me over and over. I didn't understand why he would try the experiment alone. Plus, Richard needed to be under hypnosis. In my opinion, Will just killed Richard.

The smoke finally cleared from the pod, and I leaned in to say goodbye to Richard one last time, but when I looked down at the burned corpse, I was absolutely beside myself literally because it wasn't Richard; it was me, standing right beside myself! I turned to Will and asked what was going on, but he didn't answer me. He just kept saying he was sorry. What the fuck was happening, I thought. How did I get back into the machine? I frantically panicked and screamed at the top of my lungs, but no one could hear me.

I then rushed over to Will, so I could grab him, shake him, or do something to tell me what was happening, but when I went in to touch him, my arms passed right through his body. My first instinct was I was dead. Was I? If I were dead, wouldn't I be seeing a white light? Something should be happening.

For the next hour, I just sat there with Will staring at my charred corpse. Quiet filled the basement. Just then, we heard footsteps upstairs and listened until they made it down to Will. The FBI decided to visit him. He came clean immediately on what we were doing in the basement and what those machines were. Will explained in great detail what the chambers were designed to do. I was worried that when Will explained to the FBI how many people were killed, he would be chastised for my mistakes, but there was nothing I could do.

The Feds asked Will how many times he had used the machines. What he said didn't make a lick of sense. Will swore that he had not used it yet. Will explained that this was our first test run, but something went horribly wrong when he introduced electricity to the water. The current was so strong, and when Will tried to shut it down, he encountered a problem. That is when he phoned the police. I was confused. What about all the other patients? Why wasn't Will telling the FBI about them? Samuel, Jamal, Jasmine, where were they? I then began to question myself. Where were they? Were they real? Did I even treat them? Was Will lying, or was he the only real person I had interacted with this whole time? Was I still asleep? Hours passed when I finally came to the understanding that I had died.

Every cloud has a silver lining. And mine was because everyone I thought was dead was only a dream. Jasmine was alive. I also realized later that an interesting side effect occurred. The electricity that killed me must've allowed an echo to stay behind because I followed Will home that night. I stayed beside him because I did not have anywhere else to go. Will ate, watched some tv, and then he headed to bed. Will was fast asleep, and after a few hours of staring out the window, bored to death, I decided to shut my eyes. What I observed every time my eyes shut was Will. And as they remained closed, I realized that not only could I see Will, I could communicate with him while we were sleeping. At first, I thought it was bullshit, but after a few freakish screams of me trying to convince him that I existed, he believed me. I wasn't dead. This was happening. At that moment, I convinced him that the machines had worked better than I could've dreamed. My entire life, all I ever wanted to do was help people fight back against their nightmares.

The lesson here is that you should watch what you wish for. I am not deceased. I now live with you all. Let me introduce myself. You may call me 'the Sandman'.

The end... for now.

Grab the pillow for $49.99 from Disturb Me For Art.com.

Freddy and Friends is our best seller.

CPSIA information can be obtained
at www.ICGtesting.com
Printed in the USA
LVHW040107060123
736479LV00011B/918

9 781915 852267